RAISING OLLIE

ALSO BY TOM RADEMACHER

PUBLISHED BY THE UNIVERSITY OF MINNESOTA PRESS

It Won't Be Easy: An Exceedingly Honest (and Slightly Unprofessional) Love Letter to Teaching

RAISING OLLIE

HOW MY NONBINARY ART-NERD KID
CHANGED (NEARLY) EVERYTHING I KNOW

TOM RADEMACHER

UNIVERSITY OF MINNESOTA PRESS
MINNEAPOLIS · LONDON

Published by the University of Minnesota Press
111 Third Avenue South, Suite 290
Minneapolis, MN 55401-2520
http://www.upress.umn.edu

ISBN 978-1-5179-1173-7 (pb)
A Cataloging-in-Publication record for this book is available from the Library of Congress.

Printed in the United States of America on acid-free paper

The University of Minnesota is an equal-opportunity educator and employer.

28 27 26 25 24 23 22 21   10 9 8 7 6 5 4 3 2 1

This book, and pretty much everything else I do, is for Ollie.

CONTENTS

INTRODUCTION

THE MANY STORIES OF OLIVE

WE ARE A FAMILY OF STORY HOARDERS. The things we hang on our walls and display on our shelves are pieces of stories, things we couldn't sell if we wanted to and yet would be the first things grabbed if there were a fire.

There's the small business-card–sized sign that says Cigar and Smoking in the Cognac Room Only Please from the restaurant Becca and I went to on our first big dating anniversary, still both in our teenage years. It was a place full of young people doing something fancy, and older people out for the kind of dinner you go to with a jacket on, maybe, get a steak and a few drinks. We stole the sign as our own little rebellion against the idea of going to a place like this and doing things like anniversary dinners. We were especially quirky hypocrites like that, the kind who did all the normal things ironically and still managed to do all the normal things.

There's the bright-green painting with purple and blue lines in geometric shapes, not the kind of thing we'd be into, except that this one thing is from a road trip to New York, one where our car broke in Pennsylvania and exhaust poured in through the air vents, and we got to a hotel off the highway and I promptly passed out, nearly green from breathing it in, and where Becca took a walk and got lost, but also somewhere in there found someone to come get the car, and the next day we went and talked to him, understanding very little of his thick rural Pennsylvania accent, except that there was a cheap option to just weld a thing that was, you know, not totally legal and wouldn't hold forever, or we could wait a few days for a part and pay four times as much, and seeing as we were crossing the state line that day, off we went in less than an hour.

None of that is even the story.

We got the painting because we got to New York and Becca tracked down a guy who once knew her uncle before he died and he had that painting in his back room, having hung on to it after her uncle's death just in case he ever met just the right person who should have it. That's the story.

There are mini shrines to my dad hidden all over the house. A set of beer glasses over here, this one book on the shelf, the watch on the nightstand, a little engraved pocketknife in the desk drawer.

There are all the typewriters, all with stories. My grandpa's shiny black Remington with the extra-long register because he was an engineer who needed to fit blueprints; my great-aunt's portable, a light gray Royal that clips firmly inside its own small case, that went with her to Korea and Vietnam where she was stationed as a nurse; my Great-Grandma Marie's, an olive green L. C. Smith Secretarial, the typewriter of the first writer I know of in the family, who got married in secret so Great-Grandpa Paul could go fight in World War I and she could stay and keep teaching, because married women weren't allowed to, and who wrote poems and fiery letters to the editor and little stories that the paper wouldn't publish until she started writing as P. V. Canthook, a local lumberjack. A binder of all her writing is downstairs, her own hoard of stories about Paul Bunyan that are half fables of the North Woods and half love letters to her husband. I've inherited those love letters from her, and maybe also an instinct to write them. My first book was a love letter, and this book even more so.

There's pictures, of course. Nothing professional though. No matching denim whatever and a painted sign that says Love. Instead, we have poorly taken selfies from before cameras had screens: half my face cut off on a water taxi in Sweden, everything from the nose down on both of us in Alaska, dirty and miserable and pretending to be happy that one time we went to Burning Man in the deserts of Nevada. And at our wedding, holding plastic umbrellas because the outdoor ceremony was rained out and we did the whole damn thing in a place that looked like a gymnatorium but let us bring in our own beer.

Our house was full, we thought, of all these little stories that together hold a life of stories together. It was, I mean, it *was* full, the life and the house.

And then we had Ollie, and everything got somehow more full.

I want to tell you stories, I want to tell you all the stories. But all the stories aren't mine, and all the stories aren't for you. There's a bunch of stories, though, many focused on this one, pretty big year for my family that I can share, that I'm excited to share. Like most real stories, there aren't perfect beginnings or middles or, most especially, endings. There is no clear thesis statement for any year of my life, or for any chapter of this book, but there are stories. Stories do seem to say something when they are told all together.

If I've ever taken you on a tour of my house, I'm sorry. You know that I can't tell you just one of the stories, just part of the stories. I can't tell you about the typewriters without bringing out the story binder, but those don't make real sense without the pictures of Paul's regiment, which are hung by Becca's uncle's painting and that portrait of Becca our high school art teacher painted of her as the stepmother in *Cinderella* as a set piece the summer of her junior year that we hung above our fireplace as a joke and then realized it was perfect. Piece by piece, these stories build our home.

I can't tell you about raising Olive without telling you about my dad, can't tell you about him without explaining how his illness was gasoline poured on the fire of my college-aged anxiety. I can't talk about how funny Olive is without showing you how much fun Ollie and Becca and I all have together, how, second to stories, we are a family of inside jokes and shared laughter. To tell you the story of raising Olive, I have to tell you so many stories.

These stories are satellites, orbiting each other, taking their turns in the center because the physics of stories is like that. There are the stories that started this, the bits of my childhood that have clumped together, large enough to create some kind of gravity. Stories are added from the first lurching attempts at adulthood and lost as the whole mess keeps floating wherever it's going through the cold chaos of space.

They are, all these stories now, orbiting and pushing and pushed by the mass in the middle, this thing whose speed and the weight of its importance make it shine, burning with brilliant white light. It's this most important thing I've ever done, the most important thing I'll ever do, so much that its light is changing, slightly but permanently, every other story that surrounds it. These are the stories, piece by piece, that make this book.

Piece by piece, these are the stories of raising Ollie.

And also, not to be dramatic or anything, but writing often feels like I have cut a piece of myself out from just under my ribs and nailed it to a wall, then sat back and listened to people react to it while I bleed out slowly onto the floor.

Not to be dramatic.

Writing this book has been a lot different and a lot more challenging than the teaching stuff I usually write because I've been cutting that piece out of my family, not just myself. It's tricky work, and has at times made every member of my family less than super comfortable or happy. There have been long conversations about what stories to include, and how, and how to protect everyone.

What I mean to say is, I share a lot about my family in this book, but you don't get everything, because they are more important to me than you are. I did my best to tell the stories that are mine, or from my point of view. That goes for family stories, but also personal and teaching stories. You don't get everything.

I'm a writer. I'd rather tell you everything. My wife is a therapist, which means that she, in a lot of ways, is a professional secret keeper. Her work is rooted in the protection of privacy. She'd much rather I was a writer about dragons and stuff.

We aren't a perfect family, and I think you'll see that here, but I haven't, just to make us more human and relatable, included any stories that would be deeply embarrassing or damaging, especially to Olive as they grow up.

So some stories got cut because I needed more time away from them before I could see their shape, or because I couldn't tell them without revealing stuff we didn't want to put in a book forever and ever. Sometimes I changed names or other details to protect identities, or melded a few people into one person or something like that. I didn't make up anything from scratch, though.

The essential bits are essentially true. You just don't get everything.

SCHOOL TROUBLE

WHEN OUR DAUGHTER, OLIVE, WAS SEVEN, Becca and I found out that they were probably smarter than we are. I mean, we had a pretty good idea they were pretty smart, but seven was when we started hearing it from professionals. I remember walking out of the first meeting the word *gifted* was used. It was said by a psychologist who had just finished testing Ollie, who had then taken us through the results while using phrases like "off the charts." I walked to the car thinking to myself, "Goddamn, we're screwed."

Sometimes, while we're driving, Ollie will let out a noise. I can't spell it, except to say it's somewhere between the noise of an exclamation mark and the look in someone's eye when they know for certain they're about to vomit. As parents, of course, Becca and I are always instantly alarmed and do a split-second audit of any plastic bags we may have on the floor. But, no, it's not usually anything physically wrong. The thing that bothers Ollie that severely is when they see, of all things, bad graphic design.

We have a game when we go into a store of trying to find the absolute worst logo we can. Ollie has this incredible artist's eye for color and proportion, and also a nerd's eye for font and clip-art usage. "That's the same font the tire store uses," they'll say, pointing at some off-brand juice, and they'll be right, "but it looks better for the juice," they'll continue, and they'll be right again. Then, they'll find some truly terrifying picture of a dog with human teeth smiling and say, "Oh god" as if someone just fell down the stairs in a way that looked painful but then into a mud pit in a way that looked funny. They'll demand we take a picture of the human-mouthed dog, go home, and photoshop it into a family photo, ask us please, pretty please, to frame it. We will not, but it will live on the refrigerator for a time, a memory of that one time we all laughed so loud at the grocery store we got shushed.

Olive, by the way, prefers the term *daughter,* is nonbinary, and uses they/them pronouns, and has been called Ollie or Olive interchangeably since they were a baby. Olive also prefers art to athletics, vegetables to cake, and animals to most humans. They're a bright kid who has loved school since day one but who learns, ferociously and naturally and constantly, mostly when they're anywhere but the actual school they go to every day to learn stuff.

For a lot of reasons, I really love the school Ollie goes to. It is diverse in a way that few schools in my city are, in a way that there is no racial majority in the school, and that means my daughter learns with and from kids who are recent immigrants and refugees, who speak many languages and celebrate different holidays.

Sure, they're a white kid whose closest friends are other white kids, but a few days ago we were watching *Oliver* (because their weird, mostly-white-kid choir is singing a song from it), and as we watched the scene where they were doling out gruel for the orphans, Ollie mentioned that the gruel looked like it had gelatin in it, which would mean any Muslim orphans wouldn't be able to eat it. So there's something they learned at school. Not only that, but a fact about a culture other than theirs, and that they learned not just from classmates but from their first grade teacher, who was from that culture, so that the information came with empathy. There are reasons I love their school.

In a lot of ways, though, I'm not so happy with Ollie's school. They've loved every teacher they've had and have been loved by them, but budget cuts and lack of support are hurting the kids there. Ollie tells me about how the whole second grade lunch only has one adult present, so on the day I sent them with stuff in a Tupperware they couldn't open, they didn't really eat because no one could help them.

Ollie says that bullying and behavior are problems, but because the teachers are left alone to deal with it, their focus is mainly on keeping order (which means the kids that get bullied often don't get helped). The students who most need attention and support aren't getting it until something big happens, which makes life harder for everyone, and then it is mainly a process of removal and time-outs and not addressing root causes or others impacted, or anything that will, really, make it any better the next time.

As a teacher, I get it. I've taught kids with pretty severe behavior issues. I've had times when I taught class in a hallway because a student was screaming and throwing things inside my room. As a teacher, I was glad that kid was back in my room the next week, was able to keep trying and keep growing, and that my other students got to know that student as a brilliant dancer, as wickedly funny, as able to answer any question a teacher had, but only as a response to being accused of not paying attention.

As a parent, when Ollie came home one day in first grade with a spot on their arm from being stabbed with a pencil, which they got for standing up for a friend who was being called words that even I'm not old enough to say yet, it feels different. Their first grade teacher did everything they could to take care of all those kids physically, emotionally, and intellectually, but, you know, on days when kids are getting stabbed, there's likely to be less learning.

By the next year, things were getting worse. Ollie came home with stories of kids throwing desks and chairs, of calls to the office gone unanswered as teachers struggled to handle everything alone. More and more, Ollie ended up in a corner with a book or an extra packet of worksheets, and their love of school turned to a sharp fear of the mixture of boredom and chaos of most days.

Because Ollie was identified as an advanced learner in kindergarten, they're supposed to get an hour a week with a specialist doing advanced-learnery stuff, but that person seems to be called into meetings more often than not and so can't make it. Every year seems to bring more budget cuts, more schools asked to do more with less. Also, both administrators in the building have awful reputations in the district and have been kicked around from job to job for years. I've worked with one before and was very unimpressed with, well, her basic ability to do anything. The other administrator has been described to me as "batshit crazy" by no fewer than five different people in the district in separate conversations. So, that's cool.

But all schools have their shit. I get that. I'm also finely attuned to the shit that my kid has to walk into every day.

Also, more than any of that, maybe the biggest problem we have with the school for our kid is that Ollie is bored. Excruciatingly bored.

This kid is really smart. Ollie's test scores are all in the top 1 percent of students nationally. They read and write at a level that would be passable in most middle school classrooms and, for fun, has been learning Japanese and Spanish on Duolingo while teaching themselves to code, write and record music, and edit video. We do not push Ollie to do these things. In fact, we mainly wish they would chill out now and again, but that's just not their brain.

So Ollie's bored when school is lots of worksheets and listening, and still bored when the stuff for the high-group kids is just slightly harder worksheets and listening. Bored enough that Ollie came home from school a few weeks ago and started researching advanced school programs in our area while I was making us dinner, because every second grader does that, right?

Becca asked them what a perfect school would look like, and Ollie said, "One where I got to learn all day. That would be amazing." That's a pretty low bar for any school anywhere, but one that Ollie spoke about with such longing that Becca started researching too.

So, well, shit. Now it gets difficult.

Here I thought my daughter was just a mostly sweet seven-year-old who likes video games and excruciatingly obnoxious YouTubers. Now I find out that Ollie's actually a neoliberal corporate edu-reformer bent on the destruction of public schools by weaponizing school choice. I should have known when Ollie threw out their American Girl doll and replaced it with small stuffed versions of Bill Gates, Betsy DeVos, and Michelle Rhee, started giving standardized tests to their guinea pig and doing random parent quality assessments of me ("Needs improvement").

I sat Ollie down and said to them, "Look, kiddo, I understand you wanting to choose a school that would be better for you, especially when yours isn't so great, but if you keep talking about it, people are going to hate your daddy forever and ever."

Ollie cried and cried. But they'll get over it, eventually.

Okay, that didn't happen.

Still, for someone who has often been pretty open to students and families getting to choose schools that are good for them, I've still been feeling pangs of guilt when I think about ditching the district we live in just for the little silly reason that it is making my daughter miserable.

There are a lot of things. Sure, Ollie thrives on challenging stuff and chances to think creatively and critically, but they also need adults and kids around them that understand how they think big and feel big and worry big and dream big and work big, and how sometimes doing all those things at top speed all at once can lead to big crashes.

They need a school that works to affirm their identity without making it look like work. A school that keeps Ollie safe while exposing them to new ideas, new kinds of people and places and beliefs.

Thankfully, for us and for Ollie, those places exist. Unfortunately, they aren't everywhere, and getting kids properly identified and given access to those places is not a thing we, as a whole educational system, do in a really equitable way.

We found a school for Ollie, and of course they take up a lot of the worry space in my head because they are my kid. But the process of getting Ollie to the right school and what that has meant for their intellectual growth and their happiness and health have me thinking not just about Ollie, but about all the kids out there who aren't getting that chance; about all the kids I've had and will have in my own classroom who could use some of what Ollie needs; about how I may have failed to really teach or challenge Ollie if they were in my class; about how to build a room and practice that wouldn't fail in those ways.

I mean, I hate to be the guy that's, like, "Wow, being a parent really changed me as a teacher," because I remember hearing that over and over again while I was coming up as a teacher. I remember feeling that what everyone meant was that I couldn't know what it meant to really care about kids until I had my own. Now I don't think that's exactly it.

It's not so much what you learn about kids as what you learn about yourself. Being a dad has made me a better person. Being an Olive dad, specifically, has made me think so much harder about who I am for the kids in my room and what they need from me.

Put most simply: there is nothing that has been more impactful and inspiring and important to me as a teacher than raising Olive.

MAY

THE MUSIC TEACHER

THERE ARE FEW THINGS WE CAN GET OLLIE to voluntarily leave the house for. Bubble tea is the most successful and is often used as a reward/bribe for less pleasurable things. Pokémon Go worked, like it did for the rest of the world, as a reason to actually go on a walk where there are trees and people and stuff. Then, like the rest of the world, the allure wore off, and we were back to bubble tea, swimming, and choir practice.

Though I can't promise I was any level of excited when we signed Ollie up for weekly choir practices on nights that I was the only parent home to take them, I do love that our kid loves music. They got this love, and no doubt any aptitude for it, from Becca.

The first few years of baby-having were a constant panic attack on my part. The Olive birth story is also the story of me falling apart and, at times, needing more nurse support than the freshly born baby or the woman who just freshly birthed, without any medication, a baby so big they didn't fit into newborn-sized diapers. I particularly remember one nurse yelling, "Uh-oh, Dad's gone white," and then I don't remember a lot after that for, like, a month. I am not proud.

I struggled in those early months and years to enjoy much of parenting beyond putting stupid outfits on the kid and having a reason to leave every social obligation early. I have never been less in control of anything in my life than I was with an infant who often decided to do super dumb things like not eat enough or get enough sleep, which are its only two jobs. Becca worked at night, starting shortly after my school day ended, so I had to leave work early, race home, high-five Becca on her way out the door, then spend the evening with this impossible baby that felt like a never-ending emergency. Becca, of course, was doing the same in opposite, and sleeping less because we kept pretending she could nap with Ollie during the day and so she did more of the nighttime stuff.

I remember one of those nights, trying to put Olive down to sleep, and then needing to change a diaper, but then realizing they needed a bath and new pajamas and then the diaper, and being halfway through that and hearing the dog barking from the back-yard but not wanting to pull Ollie out of the water and (obviously) unable to leave Ollie in the water alone, just trying to hurry, get-ting Ollie dried and dressed and back in their crib with the dog barking and barking and barking, and when I finally got to the back door to let the dog in, she wouldn't come. I stood in the door-way, shirt and pants wet from the bath and working on maybe five hours of sleep in the past three nights and having just taught all day and calling for the dog who wouldn't come, and then Olive started crying again, wet sobbing wails, and the dog still wouldn't come, and I sat down. Right there on the landing of the back door, just sat on the floor without the mental or physical strength to do anything else, I just sat there crying.

Except that Ollie was crying, and you don't get to give up like that when your child is crying, so I mentally scheduled my giving up for an hour or so in the future, closed the door, and walked back to Ollie's room. I picked them up, tried to rock them back to sleep, just as the dog started barking at the back door again. That was one night, but really it was kinda how the whole first year felt for me.

One thing so beautiful that it always paused my permanent-feeling panic state was listening to Becca sing to Ollie. She would fill the house with her voice, often singing Neko Case, and though I could hear it from the living room, I would get up to stand just outside of Ollie's room to listen.

I worked a bit on my own rendition of "Pure Imagination" from Willy Wonka, but I could tell Ollie, even as an infant, was doing little more than waiting until I would stop. The first few months of Olive were the most singing I've ever done and will ever do, and only when alone with a baby. I would rather stand naked in front of a group of strangers than sing in front of them, though most crowds would be equally dismayed and disappointed by either.

No, the singing is Becca's, who was a choir superstar when we met in high school (our principal actually announced the show choir as "choir athletes" at one pep rally, which shows you just how much our high school cared about/understood the arts). Becca sings in front of people because they ask her to and enjoy it, and she filled our little house with music so beautiful I often felt a little sad that Ollie and I were the only ones who got to hear.

And so it is that years later, though we can't get Ollie to happily leave the house for parties or ice cream or movies, we often leave for choir practice forty minutes early because they are so sick of waiting. It's also in a church a block and a half from our house, which means a nice short walk for Ollie to a building without a single comfortable chair for me. But they love it, and I'm willing to put up with "America the Beautiful" five times in a row to let them do this thing they love.

The outside-of-school choir is also why I assumed that the inside-of-school music class (which is mainly just choir with occasional xylophones) would be one of Ollie's favorite classes. For a time it was, or was at least very close to the top. There were songs about the water cycle in first grade, and how everyone should get along in second. Just every so often, though, a story would trickle in from Ollie about a student being sent out, or the class being yelled at or made to sit quietly for many minutes. One concert was summarily canceled because the students hadn't done enough, and it never quite got rescheduled.

The midyear-concert-that-wasn't meant that the performance at the end of the year felt pretty extra big.

This was around the time that Ollie was struggling most with school. The music teacher, doing morning duty, often talked to Becca when Ollie was getting dropped off. Drop-offs at that point were accompanied by tears, bargaining, begging. Nearly every morning, Becca would call or text me at work to let me know how it went, to process feeling awful at Ollie's fear and hatred of school. It was a tough, tough year, and sometimes the music teacher would step in and make things a little better for Ollie, telling them about the song they would practice that week or a new instrument they were trying or something, and sometimes they would simply witness, give Becca one of those "Yeah, I know" sort of smiles as she left.

Monday night choir was a bright spot, and one of Ollie's best friends from in-school music class was in the same Monday night rehearsals, so I'm sure it was just that they were singing songs from the choir, and I'm sure it was just that they were singing those songs a lot, and I'm sure it's just that they were singing those songs loudly, but one day, one of Ollie's classmates told them that their singing was bad. This is the kind of thing no one likes to hear, but is very much the kind of thing that crawls into Olive's head and sets up shop, burrowing around and knocking stuff over. (Like, I guess, a terrifying sandworm shopkeeper?) A few days later, Ollie was in music class and didn't want to sing, couldn't sing, because every time they opened their mouth that mean comment from whatever annoyed kid would pulse and throb in Ollie's brain.

That's all not wonderful enough, and one would hope—I would hope—that the teacher would notice one of her music-loving students not singing and figure out what was wrong in a helpful, supportive way. But it was only a short time till the final concert, and so I get where maybe that wasn't going to happen. Still. I mean, still, what she didn't have to do was stop the whole rehearsal, single out and embarrass Olive, and send them crying from the room. But that's what she did.

It was also even worse than all that. Ms. Music Teacher called Ollie out, asked why they weren't singing. When Ollie didn't respond, no doubt terrified as a kid who nearly never got into trouble, Ms. Music Teacher kept demanding an answer from Ollie, as the whole class looked on.

Ollie eventually found a voice to respond, saying softly, "Because I'm sad."

This is not a bad time for a reminder that this is a seven-year-old kid, a normally not only engaged but overly enthusiastic participator in Ms. Music Teacher's class.

"Well," Ms. Music Teacher said, using that voice all the kids know is her mean voice, the one she has used to break kids down before, "*you* control your emotions," she (apparently as someone who has never encountered an emotion) decided to teach Olive, "so *you* can decide to forget it and not be sad and join us, or you can decide to go, 'Wah-wah, I'm Olive and I'm sad,' and not sing." And yes, that whole "wah-wah" part was done in a faux-Olive voice and included the teacher miming rubbing her eyes and crying, "Wah-wah" like a baby. The teacher later denied this part even happened, but other kids the principal talked to who were there backed Ollie up, and also I trust my kid.

Classmates laughed, and the teacher laughed, and then Ollie, previously sad and quiet, started to cry loudly and then got upset because they were crying in front of their class, which only made them cry harder and harder until they struggled to catch their breath. Ms. Music Teacher tried, still, a little harder to explain to Ollie that they could just decide to relax, to use Ollie as an example to the class that emotions are decisions that are made and can be mastered, that Ollie just didn't want to.

Eventually, Ms. Music Teacher gave up trying to shame Ollie into breathing, told them to grab a friend and go to the nurse.

So Ollie went, played Jenga with the friend in the nurse's office till music class was over, and then went back to class. And that was it. Ms. Music Teacher never checked in again with Ollie, the small child she coaxed into crying so hard that it seemed reasonable to send them to the nurse's office; she didn't call or email me either. I heard nothing from her, or from the nurse or anyone else at the school, did not hear that this had happened to my kid until Olive, halfway home from school that day, explained why it was

maybe the worst day of school they had ever had, and did they really have to go back ever again?

I didn't even sit down when we got home before starting to type my angriest-ever parent email.

The crappy day in music class was not Ollie's first panic attack, but it was the first one we understood to be what it was. It was also the last straw in our quickly deteriorating relationship with Ollie's school that year. We went in for a meeting, but the principal explained it would be best not to "focus on the past" and wouldn't address anything that happened in the music room or what the music teacher should or could do to repair some of that damage she did. Nope, we and the principal and vice principal and music teacher all sat around the room while they asked us and Ollie what Ollie needed to do this and next year so they didn't have any more breakdowns like that at school.

I had a notebook in front of me, because it helps me in meetings to write down sentence fragments and questions to stay focused and, if I'm especially annoyed, to doodle to avoid getting very loud. The notebook page was filled with very angry little overlapping squares. Of the three of us, Ollie did the best job of asking good questions, of reminding the room that they did nothing wrong, and that if the school wanted to keep kids from having breakdowns they should probably ask the teachers not to publicly humiliate students. Becca and I fought back too, but by the end of the meeting we just let them be wrong and the worst. We knew we were leaving anyway.

There were a few weeks left in school, and Ollie spent more of them in my eighth grade classroom helping to lead activities or drawing in the corner than they did at their own school. They never went to music class again but did perform in the final concert. In the meantime, we were on the hunt for a new school.

LOOKING FOR A NEW SCHOOL

WHILE BECCA WAS PREGNANT WITH OLLIE, she had a very vivid dream about Ollie's future. In the dream, Ollie was born but still an infant. Little baby Ollie looked like a normal baby but could speak in full, complex sentences. It was a bit shocking, in the dream, but not worrisome, until a bunch of guys in suits came to the door. Whatever sensors the government had somewhere picked up our little baby genius, and they had to take the kid away now to the *Stargate* program. (I was watching a lot of *Stargate* then. I offer no excuses.) As the suits pulled Olive from the house, Olive turned to look at Becca and said, "Mom, I want to go!"

Becca woke up, told me the dream, and we laughed. When Ollie was very young, we would joke every so often about the *Stargate* program coming to take them away. As they got a little older, and in fact did start speaking in complete sentences rather early and then teaching themselves to read through iPad games, we would sometimes say, under our breath to each other, "*Stargate* Baby."

Ollie has one of those birthdays that is just on the edge of school eligibility. Technically, they should have waited an extra year before starting kindergarten, but our home district has a program where kids who are close enough can come in and test to see if they are ready. Ollie passed easily. Then, after a month or two of kindergarten, their teacher suggested we have them take the test to be identified as an advanced learner. (Everyone in the district takes the test in second grade, but the teacher saw no use in waiting.) Again, Ollie passed easily.

The *advanced learner* label didn't really mean all that much. Ollie was funneled toward a specific first grade teacher who had done some extra training (Ollie still answers without hesitation that this teacher, Ms. Abdi, is the best they've ever had), and there was a building-wide specialist who was supposed to work with Ollie and a small group of other kids once a week or so on "enrichment." Ollie was put into the high groups for math and reading, but mostly the label seemed intended for parents with a whole lot less chill than me (who obviously wouldn't at some point write a whole book about how their kid is, like, super smart and stuff).

So, yeah, Ollie was a smart kid. We were ready for that, right? Becca and I (especially Becca) were pretty smart kids, did pretty well in school. I'd taught a whole bunch of smart kids, and they all seemed to do okay. Ollie would be bored in school more often than not, it seemed, but so was I, and so were a whole lot of people. We all managed to manage.

When Ollie got old enough for bigger tests, numbers kept coming back that showed Ollie, especially in certain ways like language, sliding down the bell curve and coming to a comfortable stop where the line goes flat. So not just smart but kinda mega smart. When they took an IQ test to qualify for a school program later on, they landed on the far, far end, higher than 999 out of every thousand kids their age.

So let me say this about all of that. I don't really care. The numbers are fairly informative (and many, like IQ, are very deeply flawed) as far as what Ollie may need for schoolwork and book recommendations, but they tell me little else. I was listening to some radio interview lately where a genetic counselor was saying that very soon parents would be able to select intelligence for their child, and wouldn't they all want the highest possible? I don't know. I've known a few people with truly high intelligence, and at least in my experiences, intelligence is not a promise of happiness or even success. High intelligence actually seems to be a pretty big pain in the ass.

For Ollie, in second grade, it had started to make things pretty miserable.

Here's the thing. There's a school in another district that is specifically designed to serve kids like my kid, kids who have brains that move a million miles an hour and feel things super hard and think about things super hard, who need extra social/emotional support and challenging stuff to work on during the day. The middle school in that program just sent a bunch of instruments up in a weather balloon and then had a field trip where they followed the thing around in a school bus all day (students had to get special permission to cross state lines, just in case). I want to go on that field trip. They have a lunchroom just for introverts. I want to go to that lunch.

St. Paul has a school kinda like this, a school just for these advanced learning kiddos. I got to spend a day there, hanging out in an eighth grade social studies classroom (while we were school shopping for Ollie, but for unrelated reasons). Students came in, finding spots on couches, chairs, stools, and benches. There was a brief recap of the lesson the day before when students were introduced to a message written in code, had managed over the course of the hour to figure out for sure a few small pieces of that code, the biggest being that longer strings of letters could be broken into two-letter combinations, each that stood for a different letter. Students were reminded that they could come to the teacher with guesses and ideas and theories but would only have anything confirmed when they could present an argument with evidence why, for example, *AF* is the letter *R,* and a *VV* stands for *S.*

Some kids worked alone, some in groups. Many switched back

and forth or floated between groups as they tested their ideas out, traded information, divided labor. The teacher, Mark Westphal, was most proud about this: students had been promised a candy bar for whoever decoded the message first but, given the difficulty of the task, had decided to forgo the material prize in order to work cooperatively.

As a pedagogy geek, I was excited at the layers of things the kids were learning. This lesson was part of a World War II unit, and students had to use knowledge from previous lessons as they built the message ("But it could be January, because at that point of the war . . ."; "I don't think Britain would be sending a coded message to Japan, but maybe if . . ."). They also had a thematic goal on the board, "Critical Inquiry—Question Everything," which I wanted to tattoo on my forehead. They were all thinking and working super hard on something because it was interesting and difficult. There were a few students here or there who looked lost, waiting to collect answers from their classmates as they came together, but Mark would swing through every now and again, walk them through the process that students were using and how to start figuring it out, and they usually jumped in after that.

Lessons like this, schools like this, can be really important for students who are quick learners and intense thinkers. But also, a lot of what they do in these programs, a focus on critical, creative thinking, on academic challenge and social/emotional needs, would be good for all students. In other words, I'm not just an advocate for gifted education for smart kids. I'm an advocate for gifted education for all kids.

Some of the pace or specific content in Advanced Learner classes may not be broadly applicable to all students, and just tossing stuff at kids they aren't ready for and letting them fail can be destructive at best. I've also seen students in my own room who don't score off the charts as readers but come to life when we get

Thank you for visiting WBPL

Library name: WBWATER
User ID: 21611000100551

Title: Don't stop believin'
Author: Newton-John, Olivia,
Item ID: 31611001696431
Date due: 9/6/2022,23:59

Title: Raising Ollie : how my
nonbinary art-nerd kid cha
Author: Rademacher, Tom, 1981-
Item ID: 31611001823829
Date due: 9/6/2022,23:59

508-894-1255
M, Th, F 10-5pm
T, W 10-8pm
Sat 10-2pm

to some of the more challenging, abstract analysis sorts of stuff, often leading the entire class with their ability to critically analyze text after years of feeling behind. Too often, when students struggle with the basic-stuff worksheets, they are given more and more basic-stuff worksheets. That, or school is made "fun" in a way that is separate from learning: do this online reading program (don't get me started) for this many hours a week, and then you get extra recess or a treat or a something! Let's work for ten hours on colorful posters that show ten minutes of actual thinking! (I'm guilty of that one.)

I know my kid was miserable in a school that focused too strongly on worksheets. I also know that I would have failed second grade (because I refused to do any worksheet that I didn't think I would learn from) had my mom not intervened and negotiated a compromise. Part of Ollie's rejection of worksheet teaching has to do with how quickly my kid's brain processes stuff and seeks answers and asks questions, but no kid should be in a classroom that uses completion as a reward in exchange for the joy every damn kid feels when they work hard on something that feels like it matters or that is teaching them something important.

A few other districts around us have accelerated learner schools or classrooms, but Minneapolis does not. Minneapolis has a specialist in my kid's school who is supposed to pull them for thirty minutes a week. The district offered to let my daughter skip a grade, though they're already one of the youngest in their class. If Ollie skipped, they would have started the next year as a seven-year-old fourth grader (already overwhelmed with some of the social/emotional stresses of being a second grader). Nope. Minneapolis, quite frankly, has little more than a few different worst-case scenarios to offer us.

So there's the other school in a southern suburb. Becca took Ollie on a tour there, and every family in the tour was from Minneapolis. Same thing with a friend who toured a month earlier than we did.

Systemically, this is a problem. Minneapolis is going to struggle to build the supports it needs to build for students if its enrollment keeps dropping. It already has a bajillion dollar deficit it's currently trying to fix, which means getting rid of everything that isn't nailed down or voted in, and it means that things are not likely to get better for most kids next year anywhere. It means that to the district my child is not a priority. Ollie shouldn't be. Ollie is a middle-class white kid whose parents have the capacity to help them in many ways. They will be fine, but we're also not sticking around if we don't have to. The more that kids (and their state funding) leave the district, the harder it will be for Minneapolis. But I'm just not willing to let my kid sit and suffer in school so the district gets their money. There's a systemic answer to the problem and a personal one, and I'm always going to pick my daughter, every time, and then I'm just going to feel guilty about it.

Maybe this is the kind of school choice people feel a lot better about. I'll be staying in public schools, after all, open-enrolling somewhere else (if we're lucky enough to get in).

This opportunity is available to us as a one-kid, two-parent household with two cars. My wife is a therapist, and people don't tend to want to do therapy at 7 a.m., which means that my wife has mornings open but then also works pretty late in the evening. She can drive our daughter to school every day and can also carve out the time during the day that has allowed her to research and visit schools. Plus we make enough to afford the extra testing Ollie needed to qualify. I'm a teacher, which means I understand well enough what we were looking for and how to navigate the school system to get it.

So we have enough privilege to access a school that is right for our kid in other ways. It seems to me that much more anger is directed toward the kinds of school choice available to families without the means to drive their kid to another city every day or buy a house where the schools are more appealing to them. There's an idea that forcing the systemic answer is going to help more things get better sooner. Maybe it will, but in the meantime there are all these families in these schools that need a personal solution that their school isn't offering and so they're going to seek out the best answer for themselves. I'm never going to be mad at that.

My real worry while seeking out and switching schools is for all those other families. This works for us, for us and our kid, because we have the time to do the tours and the money for the tests and the understanding of the system to get our kid in. We have work schedules and cars that mean we can reliably drop them off at school at 9:15, and also also *also,* we have a kid who is a white kid and whose teachers saw their smarts early and looked out for them and tried to give them more and were willing to test and then trust the test that this kid needed more opportunities.

My kid is a bajillion times more likely to find themselves in a school that fits them for all these reasons. But what about those kids who aren't being identified as advanced learners because they've never been given truly challenging work? How many kids in Minneapolis (and all goddamn over) are sent to the corner with a book every day because they finished everything early and because their teacher, understandably, is spending more time with the kid who can't read than with the kid who seems to do so naturally? And how many of those kids are acting out from boredom? Or are silently very sad for much of the day, or resisting work they find to be pointless and so are treated or labeled as low achieving?

Without a place to send kids like Ollie, how many teachers even have them on their radar? If Minneapolis had a school that attracted those kids, had programs to make sure those kids were being identified early and supported in their learning, to make sure that *advanced learner* wasn't a label only applied to kids who live around the lakes, maybe fewer kids would slip by underserved.

In the meantime, what options are we giving parents who can't move close to a better school, can't drive every day to somewhere better than what's closest? What should they do? There's a systemic answer to that, and a personal one. I strongly doubt even the most fervent opponent of school choice would send their kid to a school that makes them miserable, that doesn't teach or love them enough.

I don't understand the choice debate well enough to really participate, and finding anyone willing to talk about it without shouting is difficult. Intellectually, I know every answer seems to create its own problems. But personally, I know the feeling of sending my daughter to a school they do not like and that isn't really teaching them. It's not a good feeling, and theirs is not at all a failing school, a school that is falling apart or a school where my daughter is not valued or encouraged or believed in. Ollie's is a school that doesn't work great for them, and so we found one that does.

It could be worse, but it would be great if this worked a whole lot better for everyone.

Ollie's school was fine, like, really super fine. They paid attention in class, generally, and were not a big behavior issue, generally, and had friends and were recognized for their accomplishments. But then, also, they were pretty miserable by the end of the year. They were crying on the way to school almost every day, begging to stay home. My little wonderful kiddo who used to hate weekends because they meant no school, my little kid who loves learning and doing and loves teachers and loves their classmates, hated school. Dreaded school.

This was no act, either. This was a physical reaction. To my eyes their reaction looked like anxiety or panic attacks. There was crying that could not be controlled or slowed down. There was stomach pain and sleeplessness.

The thing about my daughter, about a lot of kids like my daughter, is that the things that make them so good at tests and homework stuff also make school pretty tough sometimes. They listen to and think about every lesson from their teacher, yes, but also listen to and think about everything they hear from everyone, all day long. They makes friends easily but also feel every one of their emotions, most especially the hard ones.

Near the end of the school year, with all the crying, yes, but mostly with the increase in quiet, in sadness, in a hopelessness so outsized for a seven-year-old kid it seemed likely to consume them, we decided to bring Ollie to a therapist.

As a mom, but also as a partner and a consumer and an activist and a therapist, Becca is a researcher. It's one of the things about her I find to be most continually impressive. As baby Ollie was growing into little Ollie and proved to be more *Stargate Baby* than was comfortable, little Ollie continued to have sleep issues and trouble getting calm and trouble slowing down their thoughts. Becca started looking for people who work specifically with young kids with very active brains, and also reading every article and book she could that she thought might help.

After a hard day with younger Ollie, a day with big feelings coming out sideways at us (and more often than not, at Becca), and a nighttime bed routine lasting hours with much getting up for water, crying, getting up to go to the bathroom, back rubbing, getting up and then forgetting why they got up, stories, and anything else we could think of, I would have exactly enough energy and brain power left to decide between beer or whiskey and to put one of those things into my face. Becca, however, would pull her laptop over and start googling things, reading everything from medical studies on sleep disorders to woo-woo psychic stuff about what to do if your kid had too many ghost friends.

Oh, yeah. The ghost friends. We were worried for a while about ghost friends. Because, here's the thing, and just about anyone who's had kids can attest to this: kids say really creepy shit sometimes.

There was a time when in the middle of the night a very young Ollie was crying from their bed. Normally at this age, Ollie would be standing straight up in their crib (this is maybe a month or two away from the transition to toddler bed, which was a whole other thing). They would stand there and shout or cry for us, shocking us from sleep and screaming like someone was smashing through the door into our house (which was my most common fear since, when Ollie was only like six months old, someone tried to smash their way through our front door in the middle of the night). We would come in more than half-asleep, our mouths tasting vaguely of copper and our hearts racing, and Ollie would be screaming until they saw us, then would calm down and ask nicely for a snack, or if we could turn a small light on, or turn that same small light off, or most often help find the stuffed animal that was sitting in plain sight at the foot of the bed.

This cry, though, that time was a different cry, a new, very afraid, something-is-wrong sort of cry, and Becca nearly ran from our bed to Ollie's room, and Ollie wasn't standing, was instead curled up in the corner of the crib as if they were trying to hide.

"What's wrong, sweetie?" Becca asked.

"The man."

"The man?"

"The man in the corner over there. The man who has a head but no legs. He makes me cold." It took a while to calm them down that night, but by morning Ollie didn't even sound scared talking about it, just annoyed, you know, like how you sound when the

no-legs-standing-man is making your room cold and you just want to go to bed.

There was another time, a few months later, when they were moaning late at night. They couldn't sleep, they said. Did they need water? Or to go to the bathroom? No. It was the laughing keeping them up. I asked, "What laughing?"

"From the kids."

"What kids?"

"The children from the closet. They just keep laughing," they said, before sighing, turning over so I could rub their back, and saying, sleepily, "Oh, funny, scary children."

So I took Ollie to the car with Becca, and we burned the fucking house to the ground. As the flames hit what had only recently been Olive's room, we heard screaming, then laughing, and then, at last, silence.

Okay. So not that last part, but holy shit, would you have blamed us if we had just decided to burn it down and start over?

But no, as much as that creeped me all the way out, I don't believe in ghosts. I believe in young kids with active imaginations who are half-asleep, and also, maybe, ghosts. Becca, who definitely does believe in ghosts, had told Ollie, after reading about it somewhere else online, that they should tell the spirits in their room firmly but without yelling that they were not welcome there and to leave.

You better damn well believe I had Ollie do the firm-without-yelling thing when they told me about the scary laughing kids. Those kids had to go, especially knowing that no-legs man was still around. Ollie did and sat and watched and waited, and then said the kids were gone now, which was super good. I made sure to let Ollie know that the minute they came back, to not wait and worry about it alone, but to call right away—you know, for Becca.

The weird ghost shit was happening during a time when Olive was really sleeping poorly in general. There were times that they kinda half-woke up and would be moaning or yelling in their sleep and we couldn't wake them up right away. Fun. There were times they didn't fall asleep until after midnight and would be completely awake by 4:30 or 5:00 in the morning. Double fun. There were other times that they would be up in the middle of the night for an hour or more, sometimes multiple times a night, just couldn't keep their body still or were fighting sleep like crazy because they were scared of the nightmares they kept having. All the fun!

You know when you're younger and the first member of your friend group has kids, and they tell everyone else that they should have kids too? They don't tell you about no-legs man. They probably made a deal with no-legs man that he would move to your house once you had kids.

Becca did a lot of reading online (creepy things kids see/hear/

say is quite the rabbit hole), introduced some safety mantras, and for a few nights would walk around the house ringing bells because she read somewhere that doing so drove spirits away. She also looked into night terrors and sleep schedules, and we implemented new bedtime rituals (slowly, because routine change is tough on Ollie). She also took Ollie to a psychic who told Ollie that, on their way traveling to their own dreams, Ollie was getting distracted by the nightmares of others and would enter their dreams to help but then get trapped. The psychic taught them a visualization involving filling their feet with light or something, and affirming before bed, "I will dream my own dreams." The spiritual stuff worked as well (or better) than the sciency stuff, and things got better bit by bit.

I would have been lost through this, through many of the big transitions, without Becca, because I do not try to fix things.

So one time, and maybe this story is too long to tell, or to tell completely, but I was biking to work in the morning and a car hit a deer and flung the deer into my bicycle, which then flung me, going rather fast down a hill, onto the road. I tore up my pants and my gloves and was bleeding from a few different places. The woman who was driving got out, ran to the deer, said, "Oh, thank god, I thought it was a dog," and then left while I was still lying there. Someone else stopped and called the cops, who came and checked on me and then shot the deer right in front of me without warning, right there in someone's suburban front yard. A coworker picked me up, and I did my best not to bleed in her car on the way to school, then went right to the school nurse, who cleaned me up a bit and taped bags of ice around both my palms, and I spent the day walking around like a broken baby raptor.

I still worked that day because I'm dumb, and my right shoulder, which took the brunt of the impact, hurts kind of a lot fairly often. However, other than having multiple doctors and bodyworkers tell me that there are things in my shoulder that are no longer in the right place, I've never done anything to fix it. I keep thinking it will get better on its own. This was, now, oh, ten years ago. My shoulder hurts right now.

I apply this truly abysmal strategy toward life and fixing problems to many things. Becca does not, which is why I still have nice things and why I went to get massages in the first place, and also why Olive slept better with less nightmares, and why Olive starting seeing a therapist when they really needed to (goddamn, that was quite the aside, but we're back to therapy now), and why that therapist's recommendations led to many hours of working and researching and questioning and finally deciding to move Ollie to this whole other school.

Ollie was super nervous that first time walking into therapy and then looked forward to it every time after. As parents we knew in the first few minutes of the first session (we all sat in on that first one, Ollie would kick us out after quick check-ins during later sessions) we had made the right choice. It took the therapist a few quick questions to Ollie before nailing down pretty quickly the kind of kid that Olive is. Do you learn new things easily? (Yes.) Do you remember almost everything, big and small? (Yes.) Do things in school go too slow sometimes? (Big yes.) Do you get upset when other people break the rules? (I am upset just thinking about it now.)

The therapist introduced us to the idea of Intense kids (when talking to Ollie, she usually says "bright kids"). Ollie checked every box there was to check. Intensity, in this context, means a kid who learns intensely, thinks intensely, feels intensely, processes intensely. It kinda sounds like a lot, and I imagine it is, and the term put together a whole lot of pieces of Olive for us. I mean, a lot of that is pretty common kid stuff, and with Ollie it's just super common kid stuff turned to full volume all the time.

The therapist went on to explain how a lot of kids in kindergarten may be taught that, say, a cat is an animal. Their brain will take that piece of information (cat) and put it inside a little box in their head (animals) and then be ready for the next bit of learning. Bright kids, she told us, would be told a cat is an animal and then ask themselves how many categories there were besides animals, and how different a cat would have to be in order to not be an animal. Ollie jumped in without prompting, wondering if cats could communicate with each other and if so, is there a cat dictionary, and if so, wouldn't it be cool to have one, and it would probably be even bigger than a person dictionary because they have to communicate things so quickly and so would need really specific words. The therapist looked from Olive to us and smiled.

In fourteen years and more than a thousand students, I've taught and known and loved a whole lot of kids who present somewhere on the Autism Spectrum. I'd noticed some things consistent with that with Ollie, especially in their sensory stuff. Clothes had to be a certain way, made of certain things, and big loud places and loud noises impacted Ollie more than a lot of kids. Though we wouldn't be upset if Olive is autistic, intensity matches Ollie's person a whole lot better, and understanding it gave us a lot more information about what Ollie needed in a school.

At the same time that we were doing all the searching and testing and applying that went into finding a new school for Ollie, I was looking for another new school for me.

Two years before, I had left a job I was really not good at as an instructional coach (which meant going into classrooms and watching other people teach and then telling them things they may want to try differently and being mostly ignored and spending the rest of the day in meetings with other people talking about the work that other people are doing). I'm supposed to be in a classroom anyway.

Really. I'm not good with adults. Like, my principal at the coaching job refused to meet with me for five months straight because I kept asking her if I could work with kids more. When she finally did meet with me, she told me my funding had shifted and I actually wouldn't be working with kids at all. Instead, I was to have a grant-funded position as a full-time coach for only five teachers. I would work with them all day on lesson planning and conflict-resolution strategies and trauma-informed practices but would not be able to work with their students directly at any point. Yuck.

So I went back to the place I started, an arts and racial integration magnet school just out of the city. There were lots of familiar faces, a few people who really got me, which had been very often not true in the years prior. The school had a structure and philosophy I knew well, and the struggles that had kinda always been our struggles.

It was on balance a good year. I felt at home, felt like I could probably be there the rest of my career.

Then I got fired.

Well, okay, I didn't get *fired*-fired. The district, and stop me if you've heard this one, was having a budget crisis. Because my weirdo magnet district of two schools had dissolved and given their schools to other districts, my first year back at my old school was actually my third year straight in a different district. Also, I was hired very near the start of the year, which would make me, you know, one of the last in, which also made me one of the first out. They really tried to keep me, actually, at least the building administration did, but in the end I was cut and was suddenly looking for a new job.

This is where the story gets a little weird and I have to step to the side of my usual "just-an-aw-shucks-normal-teacher" vibe. I had been a Minnesota Teacher of the Year a few years before and released my first book during the year I was cut. The news found it to be a pretty interesting story that a Teacher of the Year had been cut from his job. Lots of people wanted me to jump in as the poster child against the Last In First Out policies that got me canned and against ideas of seniority and tenure in general. I wasn't into it. The story to me was that so many teachers in the district as a whole were being cut when what we really needed was more teachers with better support. The story, I believed, was that we were headed away from what our kids needed, which was a story no one wanted to tell.

A few days after I found out I was cut, a student came directly from their bus to my room, sneaking past the hall monitor who was supposed to keep students in the cafeteria until ten minutes before class. Their parent had the news on that morning, and there was a segment (one I had no idea was happening) talking about how I was getting fired. I hadn't told my classes yet, trying to grab a few days first to process it myself, but here we were.

Within the next few days, both major papers in the area had stories, and my joblessness was a segment replayed on public radio every hour on the hour for a day. I declined something like seventy different interview requests, local and national, because I kinda didn't want to, because it sucked to get kinda fired.

Soon after the stories started, the emails and messages started coming in. Teachers and principals from around the area who knew me or knew of me were wondering if I'd like to send a résumé their way, that this or that job was opening and they'd love to talk to me. This is not a thing that usually happens to teachers, but it should. If we did better at celebrating teachers when they did truly great work, then teacher recruitment would mean a lot more than posting a job on your website and seeing who shows up.

If I had to leave, I was really hoping to get back into the city. The city unfortunately wasn't hiring, since they were cutting more jobs than they were opening. Also, because big-school bureaucracies are awesome and definitely the way to go, there were principals with job openings they would have loved to offer to me but weren't allowed to because I had to go through the district hiring pool, but the person who ran the hiring pool had been—I'm not kidding—cut, and so no one was forwarded those résumés.

Meanwhile, I was hearing from schools who had the freedom to be more flexible and more forward with their job offers, which meant mainly wealthy exurban districts and charters. I sent a lot of "sounds interesting, currently not looking to commit to a job just yet" emails.

I like to walk. It's a way I handle stress and anxiety and a brain that never stops, and walking helps to curb my desire to handle those things by looking at dumb things on screens. I pop in headphones with a podcast or lo-fi hip-hop and walk for miles, taking random turns and getting myself lost and refound. It is one of a very few things I do to try to take care of myself.

I was on one of these long walks, taking the opportunity of a two-hour choir rehearsal of Ollie's to walk in a random direction for an hour, then turn around and walk back, when I got a direct message on Twitter from someone I follow but didn't really know. She was a principal of a school of a teeny district cut out of the northeast corner of the city. "Mr. Rad, you don't know me. I'm a principal with an eighth grade LA [language arts] job opening next year. Interested?" Before I answered, I scrolled through her timeline and found all sorts of stuff about antiracist research and pictures of goofy kids doing goofy stuff and her, for some reason, riding a bike through the hallways of the school. Not only that, but she had seen me call for the burning down of everything awful, seen me swearing all the time and saying all the things I think

Twitter is for, and she still messaged me. I figured that was worth a "totally interested" response.

"Google the school, read about us. We love kids, all of them." Worth a phone call. She was free then, and I was just walking, so we talked as I wandered with not so much a destination as a time I was walking toward. I hit the hour mark and turned around, still on the phone, and headed back to choir. She didn't try too hard to sell the school, focusing instead on the work that needed to be done.

A policeman in the town had killed Philando Castile that year. The school pretty much shared a parking lot with the police station, a place that had been a gathering point for protests and support rallies against the officer through the year. Neighbors announced ideological battle lines using Black Lives Matter or We Back the Blue yard signs, and the tension was bleeding into the hallways of the middle school. A group of seventh grade girls of color had started a diversity leadership group, had invited officers from the station to walk over and share pizza and perspectives, and were coming up against friction from some white families and white students.

The principal talked about the need for more teachers of color, of course, but also more white allies who could model what it meant to be a white dude who listened to people of color. This sounded like good work to me.

She said she wanted teachers who would do big crazy projects that focused on authentic learning and critical thinking. The school had been stuck for too long in its traditions, in ways of teaching that served a lot of their white kids well enough but was too comfortable letting kids of color, kids getting special services, and any other kids less interested in "playing school" fall behind.

"You'd have my blessing to come fuck shit up," she said in our very first phone conversation together. Worth a school visit and an interview, for sure.

It's a weird place, this school. There are two highway exits that get you there. One goes through a big-box shopping center-y place that serves the northeast part of the city. I'd been there a million times when I lived nearby during college, and it still feels like Minneapolis. The school is like five minutes past that. The second exit, the exit I took the first time I drove to the school, takes a windy road with a golf course on one side and a cemetery on the other. I drove around, looking for signs of, I don't know, coolness, and instead found myself wondering how many old dudes had basically moved from one side of the road to the other, and if they (or anyone else) noticed.

I drove past the scripty-letter town sign with a little shudder and nearly turned around when I hit the corner of the school and saw the town's big spraying fountain.

I'm a weird sort of snob. Things that look too nice make me feel uncomfortable. People who act too nice make me uncomfortable too, which meant that the two people out walking dogs who waved randomly at my car as I drove up to the school did not help.

The three houses directly across from the school all had We Back the Blue signs pointed right at the school. I wondered about the kids of color inside, kids who had seen the Philando video over and over, and if those signs, in this place and during this year, could well have read "He deserved it" to them.

In my interview, and in small meetings I joined in on during the summer, I found a group of adults doing cool work. It's a middle school whose intentions are to allow its students to be middle schoolers, to support them and challenge them and help them grow, and also delight in their ability to be the kinds of dummies that eleven-to-thirteen-year-olds very often are. It's a school a few years into real racial equity work that has been dropped headfirst into the deep end of the pool. It's a school in a community with a whole bunch of what was described to me by one support staff member as "old-school whites," as well as a large Tibetan population, and more actual racial and cultural diversity among the other forty or so percent of the population that is kids of color than any other place I've worked in.

I knew there were cool things going on there, good people working there. I also knew, walking into the school and seeing club signs and mascot murals and framed photos of an entirely white staff, that there was going to be stuff that was weird. This felt like the school I went to in middle school. I hated my middle school. Now I work there.

After eleven years of teaching at art schools, schools founded on racial desegregation, schools that served large numbers of kids from marginalized communities, and no matter how much I talk about how close it is to downtown, about the work and the kids and everything else, I had to face the facts.

I now taught in the suburbs, and I had no plan how to do that well.

JULY

IN DENVER

BEFORE THE STRESS OF NEW SCHOOLS started, we took a family road trip to Denver. The trip was exactly what we all needed, especially Ollie. Every mile we drove away from home, away from that year in school, seemed to bring a little life back to them. Every new adventure on the trip (except maybe Wall Drug, which was useless) was a memory that pushed the anxiety-filled boredom, and the teacher making crying eyes in front of the class, a little further away from the front of Ollie's mind.

A child of their generation, Ollie was accustomed to car rides that featured many glowing screens of videos, games, and various art-related apps. But on that trip, the longest car ride we'd ever taken, a trip that included driving through some of the more beautiful spots in our country and also Nebraska, Ollie left the iPad in its case most days. They looked out the window, sang along to *Hamilton,* played round after round of Would You Rather, and tried to spot license plates from every state (we got them all, even Hawaii twice, you know, not to brag or anything).

Every so often, Ollie would spend time quietly staring out the window, lost in their thoughts. They would occasionally turn to us and ask a question. Sometimes it was about what would happen if a person ate only breadsticks for a year, or whether we thought they could build a car that ran like a music box, and what song would be the most popular for a car engine. Sometimes they would ask questions about the new school next year, about what we thought about all the things that happened at their old school, about why the music teacher didn't understand how to help them, and how hopefully the teacher did now so that students next year wouldn't get treated like that. We'd answer, chat a bit, and then Ollie would go quiet, the little gears and springs and windy things turning away in their head almost visible in the reflection of their eyes against the car window.

Becca had a conference to attend in Denver but pushed for the full family trip because she had wanted to show our child the Corn Palace since before we had a child. Look, I'm never divorcing Becca—she's too wonderful. But if I did divorce Becca, the very first line of my case would mention her love of roadside attractions. If she ever divorced me, the first line of her case would mention how funny I think I am.

The most successful stop of the trip was to yet another roadside attraction called 1880 Town, which is a fake Old West town built on a big flat field. Also, there's a fifties-style diner in a train car in the parking lot, you know, because. Becca loved it before we ever even got there. Ollie was actually game for the whole thing, though they spent more than half the time chasing around a few cats that lived amongst the two cows you could pay to pet.

There was a little shop where you could rent costumes, which Becca made a beeline for upon entering. No point in being in 1880 Town and not dressing the part, right? My worry was that dressing up would only further encourage my very least favorite thing in the world, which is people attempting to interact with me while they are in character and expecting me to play along. Becca was looking through all the big frilly dresses, from adult to child sized, and asked Ollie if they wanted to dress up too. They looked at the dresses like they were made of eyeballs, disgusted to the point that they felt they needed to apologize to the woman who owned the shop for their reaction. It was right around that time that I was feeling just how crowded the shop was with old dusty costumes and people and excused myself to a rocking chair I had spotted just outside the door (likely placed there specifically for grumpy dads like me).

Ten glorious paid-actor-free minutes later, Becca and Ollie emerged. Becca had on a dress that was a frilly explosion of purple nonsense and was followed by just about the most perfect little western sheriff I had ever seen. Becca saw my surprise and explained, "Ollie saw the sheriff outfit and really wanted to wear it." They had tucked their wavy long hair under a black cowboy hat. A brown leather vest (with badge, obviously), a red bandanna tied around their neck, and a low-slung gun belt finished the outfit, and they spent the day swaggering around and pointing orange-tipped silver pistols at imaginary train robbers and posing for pictures and selfies making cartoonishly large winks in front of old-timey stuff. When the costume was finally returned and the long hair came back out, they somehow looked a little less like themselves than they did when they were playing cowboy.

We camped the whole way out, one night on an air mattress that failed to the point that we could feel the ground against our butts with our heads two feet in the air, one night at a place that insisted we put all our food in a special lockbox because bears had been smashing car windows, and another night during a storm with winds so strong they almost pushed the ceiling of our tent against us.

So when we got to Denver, to the hotel that featured a bathroom without spiders, beds that stay where you put them, and pizza delivery, I was all set for a few days of laying around with Ollie while Becca went to work.

On our first morning there, Ollie was unwilling to order pizza for a third straight meal, so we walked down the street to get some bagels. While we waited in line to order, a whole group of Teenage Mutant Ninja Turtles walked in with lanyards around their necks. As we looked at them, we saw Wolverine walking by with about fifteen Deadpools, an Egg McMuffin in every hand.

"Dad. DAD. DadDadDadDadDad. I think there's a Con happening." They said this, like, I don't know . . . there's nothing in the world like a nerd in the presence of other nerds meeting to do nerd stuff, so it sounded just like that.

We could have asked, of course, any of the costumed people around us, but neither Olive nor I is ever very interested in talking to a stranger when something can be Googled. Sure enough, Denver Comic Con was happening, just two blocks away. Ollie was a fan of nearly every aspect of nerd culture, starting with an obsession for *Steven Universe,* a show about a young awkward boy trying to find superpowers, which was also a show about the fluidity of gender and the strength of many different kinds of love, and also monsters get punched in the face and stuff. There's much deeper lore to the world of the show, and Ollie knows it all, absorbing it on watches and rewatches of the series. They've also started gaming, preferring 2D games like Undertale that look like games from my childhood but feature sharp humor, a gender-fluid main character, and a huge community of online nerdery devoted to its worship. Ollie loved all these things and more, collecting new fandoms from friends at school and YouTube rabbit holes. A Con was very high on the wish list, just under a trip to Japan.

I'd never been, but the timing was too perfect to pass up. I made them promise to help me get our laundry done and clean out the car (which appeared to have lived through the last thirty minutes of a *Mad Max*–style postapocalyptic movie where the only food available was found at gas stations), and then we would spend as much time as they wanted during the following day going to nerd fest.

The line to get in the next day took us an hour to get through, an hour that Olive had almost no trouble with, as they spent the time spotting cosplays from various obscure *Steven Universe* fan favorites, anime series I don't know about, and characters from Undertale. While we waited, I looked through the convention app on my phone, found appearances of celebrities and creators that we could go to, panels of actors talking about some aspect of fandom. Honestly, there were some pretty cool ones, some pretty big names. I kept rattling them off to Ollie, who was wholly uninterested in them. Okay, so maybe the marketplace that has tons of games and toys and gifts and stuff? Meh. Maybe later. So what's first?

"Artists' Alley."

Oh, yep, there it is, at the back of the bottom floor. This isn't where the big-name comic artists go, because they have their own section with big booths and signings and all that. Artists' Alley is for independent artists and DIY crafters who set up shop to sell their stuff. A large portion of it is fan art, their interpretations of beloved characters and imagined crossovers (there was some pretty cool *Hamilton/Star Wars* posters). Okay, so Ollie wanted to start there, see some artists arting. It was two aisles long, and I figured we'd be done in about a half-hour. We stayed for eight hours. Eight full hours, looking at art, talking to artists, asking questions about the artists and their art, spending a few hundred dollars on all the things that just must be had.

We took one break, for lunch, and Ollie spent that time on their iPad drawing. It reminded me of those artsy kids who went to poetry readings and coffee shops and spent the time writing their own poetry (I am guilty of this). Well, Ollie was a lot less obnoxious than that. They were just so, so excited.

Ollie had been teaching themselves how to do digital art, watching YouTube art tutorials and stuff, and practicing often on a three-year-old iPad I had gotten for work and was instantly claimed by our young screen hog. Unbeknownst to me, Ollie had been researching different kinds of drawing pads they could get that would help them draw better and more complex things. Now, surrounded by digital artists, they had questions.

Every artist got pretty much the same grilling. What kind of software did they use? What kind of hardware? If the artist were starting over now, what would they buy first?

So one of the things that made this experience so great, and one of the reasons we bought so much stuff, is that these artists were incredibly giving of their time and talent and suggestions to Ollie. Many pulled out their various iPads and drawing tablets and let Ollie try, especially when the artists' answers mentioned a program being "easier" because Ollie's a kid and Ollie responded with non-kidlike questions about layering, 3D modeling, and a whole bunch of other terms that flew thirty feet over my head. It's a weird experience, hearing your seven-year-old talk with another adult and not understand most of what they're talking about because it's far too technical and advanced.

Ollie took the lead, picking and choosing which artists to stop and talk to. We stopped at every single artist who presented as female. We ran to any artist who appeared to be queer or gender nonconforming in some way. On the way out of the Con that evening, I asked if Ollie had intentionally skipped every male artist there. "There were male artists there?" Ollie was not kidding. Had totally missed them. I would guess that about 80 percent of the artists there were dudes, but to Ollie they were just background to the brilliant work that everyone else was doing.

My job was not to steer Ollie toward anyone or really engage in the conversations. That much became clear rather quickly. My job was to start the conversation because Ollie was too shy (or, as they put it, scared of being awkward) to do so. I would say hello, would introduce Ollie as a burgeoning digital artist, and usually before I finished that sentence, Ollie would jump in and start asking questions about all the things. I would stand quietly behind, waiting for the second part of my job, which was to pay for something. It seemed only fair to buy something in exchange for their time. Plus, you know, so much of it was so cool and now lines the walls around Ollie's art desk (which they almost never use, because they'd rather draw on their bed or the couch or the hammock chair on the porch or anywhere that isn't the very nice place we set up for exactly that purpose).

When we went back to the hotel that night, Ollie begged to be allowed to start their own artist Instagram. Everyone there had one, and many had suggested it as a great tool for networking and getting your art out there. I folded easily, with rules around using it for art and not pictures and not making any works of art that consisted of, like, the address of our home or anything like that. Ollie started it that night, followed the artists they had spent the day talking to. Many of them followed Ollie back, and some have continued to comment on Ollie's posts and show support for years after.

Ollie came home from that trip on fire. We started taking trips during the day to coffee shops so they could sit and draw and I could sit and write (I mainly spent time on my computer getting in fights on Twitter about stuff I've since forgotten but that at the moment, I'm sure, felt very important). On one of those trips, we went to our local cat café. (One room is a coffee shop; the adjoining room is full of cats that can be adopted. For a less-than-small fee, you can spend half an hour in the room full of cats. This room is why Olive will not be allowed to have a credit card until they are forty.)

Ollie sat across from me at one of the tables, an untouched iced tea and cookie in front of them, and did a series of ink and watercolor drawings of the cats in the other room. One drawing, my favorite, pictured all the cats together wearing funny hats and had the words *cat party* written above. Ollie posted them to their Instagram, and I shared them on my Facebook so family could see. Before we left, we had three people asking if Ollie could do drawings of their cats, saying they would be willing to pay.

"My first commission!" Ollie screamed loud enough to disturb the cats in the next room. When we got home, they went to work. They spent the summer doing all sorts of commissions for people, of their pets mostly, but also family portraits and other art. Most were done with ink and watercolor, kinda because Ollie didn't have the right digital stuff yet, and kinda because a lot of the artists at the Con told Ollie that they should keep practicing doing nondigital art because it would be good for them as an artist.

Ollie drew a ton that summer, usually asking for a dollar or two per picture and usually getting between five and ten. By the end of the summer, they were able to combine their earnings with money intended for their birthday presents and bought themselves a new iPad, an Apple pencil, and the drawing software ProCreate (most everyone in Artists' Alley had suggested this combination).

One of the neat things ProCreate does is build a sort of time-lapse video of a drawing as you create it. Watching these videos of Ollie's art is consistently awe inspiring. Their command of the program, using one hand to zoom, turn, flip, and access tools while using another to draw, creating a sketch layer and inking it in carefully, trying this sort of line stroke, then another, playing with color and form and perspective, and then finishing with these pieces that look, to my eyes, like the single, most impressive pieces of artwork ever on the planet. Ollie posts these videos to their Instagram every so often, and I watch them over and over. As someone who has never done visual art in any serious way, who has no natural eye for color or shapes, it all looks like magic to me.

In addition to the iPad, there were only two things that Ollie really wanted for their birthday. Every year before this, Becca had sewed Ollie a dress for their birthday. Their first birthday dress was blue and sparkly and had a felt owl and star from Ollie's favorite YouTube version of "Twinkle, Twinkle, Little Star" that had Velcro on the back and could be moved around. The year before this, Ollie had designed their own dress, a white frilly thing with a rose that wound up the side. This year, Ollie wasn't interested in a dress and asked instead if Becca would help them make their first full cosplay. Becca outdid herself, and with faux-gold buttons and piping, tall brown boots, and a blue fitted long-coat, we had a rather convincing-looking Hamilton for the day (and any day after they could think of an excuse to wear it).

The other thing they asked for, which went well with the costume, was a haircut. Specifically, they wanted their hair short enough to style into a mohawk when they wanted to, or kinda sweep to the side when they didn't, and the sides and back of their head shaved close. We took them to this stylist right by Becca's office, overlooking the park where the Twin Cities' Pride Fest was just beginning to set up tents and stages. The guy who owned the shop was an old rockabilly-type who sells vinyl in the room next to where the hair is done. (Or at least he has them available for sale. I've never seen anyone actually shopping there.) He started by putting Ollie's hair into a ponytail, taking scissors, and snipping the whole damn thing off. I actually expected Ollie to cry, but no, they saw him hold the ponytail up and let loose a triumphant "Aww, YEAH!"

When we left the shop, we had Ollie stand in front of some big green plants nearby. They were wearing an olive-green jean jacket, white tank top, jeans, and sneakers to go with their newly shaved and styled hair.

You know those magic eye posters they used to have in the mall? The idea was you would stare and stare at them, through all the blurs and noise and shapes, but only when you relaxed your eyes just right, a crystal-clear image would emerge. It was just a haircut, sure, but in that moment Ollie looked more clearly like themselves than I had ever seen.

OPEN HOUSES AND KIDS LIKE ME

IN THE SUMMER BEFORE OLLIE'S MOVE to the new school, we drove past once or twice on Ollie's suggestion, just to go see it. One day, some of their worry surfaced. "At the new school," they asked, sincerely, "do you think there will be more kids like me?"

"Nerds?" I responded, helpfully. "Yeah, there will be lots."

"No." They gave me that look they give me when they're giving me that look: "Like, sometimes kids last year cried when something big happened, but I cried sometimes when other kids didn't." I remember some of those times, when Ollie would come home and tell us that they were given a warning for coming in a few minutes late from recess (because their friend forgot their coat on the other side of the field and they went with them to get it), and how that very mildest of reproaches led to them crying for twenty minutes or more in the hallway, partially about the injustice of being "in trouble" for helping out a friend, and partially because they were crying and felt like they shouldn't be crying.

So Ollie was asking specifically about the crying thing, about getting overwhelmed and feeling things really intensely a lot of the time. They were also asking about, you know, just kids like them. Kids who learned things really quickly, who liked to learn about a lot of different things very deeply, who liked to embrace expressions of that learning. So, you know, nerds.

I didn't get to make it to Ollie's first event at the new school, which was a gathering at a park to pick up schedules and meet the principal and run around and stuff. It fell on the night of open house at my new school, which was a gathering in the park outside our school where teachers stood in chalked-off circles by subject area and students had a little passport they walked around with for you to sign.

Ollie, unlike me, has never really struggled to make friends. However, Ollie, like me, gets especially quiet and weird during big events with lots of people where there is an expectation that you will make a lot of friends. So there was more social anxiety than excitement for their gathering, and Ollie was only convinced to go after being promised that no one would force them to talk to anyone, and it would be a good thing if they just saw some of the kids they'd be in school with, and that afterward they could get bubble tea.

I don't always love things like open houses. Actually, yeah, I usually hate them, even though they can be important sometimes, I guess, you know, to meet families and nervous kids and all that. My first open house at the new school was going fine, if not a little boring and exceptionally awkward. The Language Arts teacher in the grade below me was pretty new to teaching, and young, and had been joined nearly all week by her boyfriend. He sat in her class during staff meetings and stuff but was otherwise around, mostly not doing anything other than being around. At one point I wandered into her room to see if she had a staple remover (for whatever reason, though they're inexpensive, every school seems to only be allowed to have three in the whole building), and she was sitting on his lap at her desk. It was weird.

At the open house he stood inside the little chalked-in circle with the other Language Arts teachers. There are only four of us, total, and two of us were new to the school, so he ended up explaining to nearly every family that, no, he didn't work there. The teacher joked with me at one point that her boyfriend should get a badge that says "Not an employee," and I thought, yeah, that would be, you know, one option.

About an hour into the open house, the sun had moved to a position in the sky where it was somehow exactly always in my eye. I ran off to my car to get my sunglasses (and to get away for five minutes from dude who was continuing to dude) and rejoined the team. The sunglasses were pink. On our road trip, I let Ollie pick out sunglasses at a gas station for me, and they picked the brightest bright pink ones. It turned out that they fit my face perfectly and were just the right kind of springy and kinda soft and perfect. I loved the sunglasses, even bought a glasses repair kit that cost more than the glasses did. Anyway, yeah. The point is, the sunglasses were pink, which is neither interesting nor edgy as far as I understand it. Over the course of the next hour, however, many people would disagree.

One mom said, "Hun, did you see your teacher's sunglasses?" to her mortified teen and later told me that my glasses had suggested to them I was likely to be a safe space for their gradually-coming-out kid. The power of pink.

Most people mentioned that they *really* loved my glasses or said a simple "Nice glasses," or something like that, but always with a tone and a look that said, in my head, in the voice of an Old West sheriff, "Just who the hell do you think you are, wearing pink in this here town?!"

It was a little thing. It was just pink glasses. It was also one of the first signs I had that the people around me were not necessarily my people. This is not to say that I'm cooler or better or anything than any of the people I work with and around; I just didn't feel, especially that first year, like I really fit in.

This isn't a feeling that was wholly new to me, either. I went to high school in one of the most normal-ass high schools in the world, in a normal-ass city in normal-ass Wisconsin. The school was mostly affluent and nearly entirely white. I'm also really super white, but my family was far from being wealthy. More than that, though, I just never fit into the football game–school dance–junior business vibe of my school. Where most kids fit comfortably into an informal dress code that could be called upper-middle-Abercrombie, I was dying my hair pink, wearing skirts and eye makeup and nearly anything else I could think of to shout "I don't belong here" every day. I had a small group of theater nerd friends that welcomed me in, but on the whole our existence was defined by how unwelcome we were everywhere we went.

When I got to college, the guys next door in the dorms and I became friends and got an apartment the next year. They were a rapper and a DJ, part of a larger hip-hop group that performed often and was doing well enough they stopped doing the whole school thing to focus on music. Our apartment was one of the places that people in the Minneapolis rap scene hung out in. I got into hip-hop but still listened to Phish in my headphones and was the only one there actually going to classes and doing homework. They were my friends, for sure, and their art made me want to do my art better, but especially when there were big groups of other rap dudes around doing rap dude things, it's hard to say I was fitting in.

So here I was, the odd man out of a staff I didn't really know yet. Okay, fine. Ollie, however, was having the very opposite experience. On my dinner break, I decided to go get some quiet in my room and checked my phone while eating. There was a text from

Becca: "First kid Ollie saw was wearing a whole space suit. Ollie ran right up to her, they've been playing together for an hour already."

Making friends has never been super challenging for Ollie. There was one year that they were in a summer day camp, the kind, like nearly all summer day camps we've found, that is a ridiculous mess of a very specific focus or activity that will keep no one's attention all day, a whole bunch of fun-activity-for-kids stuff from Pinterest, and one fewer college kid than really needed for whatever the size of the group is. Ollie kept coming home talking about this kid that was just like them, this new friend.

"What's her name?"

"Ugh. I dunno. I keep forgetting to ask." I don't know if this is all kids, but this is definitely Ollie, who will (and in this case did) invite a child to our house for a birthday party before learning said child's name. The child accepted the invite, but seeing as they were both six or so, we figured it was a good time for adults to step in. We sent a written invite with parent contact info on it. (I swear, for a time there, I was thinking about making business cards on them that announced me as "dad of Ollie" and gave a phone number, email, and good key terms for internet research on me before deciding if our kids could be friends.) Ollie came home upset.

"She wasn't there today," they complained. "She went with her family on vacation and won't be there the whole rest of the week."

"And she didn't say that before?"

"No, she did. I just kept forgetting." Again, I don't know if this is all kids. Probably, though.

So we sent an email to the people running the camp and asked if they would pass it on to the parents of the child who was there that week and playing with our kid but who now was gone and whose name we did not know.

A week later, I got an email from one of my literary heroes, a man who had, a decade before, convinced me for a short moment that I enjoyed watching spoken word poetry (such was his skill), and who was in many ways a writing giant and genius. I figured the email was one of those, "Hey, TOM, I wanted to tell you about this really important literary organization that could really use your money. Wasn't it kinda cool seeing my name in your inbox? Surely, that's worth *something*." But, no, it was a real email, from him to me. Well, mostly it was to Ollie, apologizing that his kid couldn't make it to the birthday party, but maybe they could plan a time soon to hang out?

And that was the start of one of Ollie's many strong friendships.

And though my first open house at my new school was not full of famous writers' kids who wanted to be my friends, or even a single person in a space suit, there was one person who seemed to have come just to get to meet me.

While I was sitting having my dinner in my still mostly empty room, one student's dad came up to me at my desk carrying a thickly stuffed manila folder.

"Hello! I'm Mr. Rademacher, I'll be teach—"

"I know who you are. Do you know who I am?"

"I do not. Do you have a student with me this year?"

"Yeah. I'm surprised you don't know me, though," he said, as if he was calling me out on a lie, because obviously I would know him. "I'm sure the principal has talked to you about me."

"Umm . . . nope. She hasn't, but anyway, I was just finishing up my dinner and I'll be right out—"

"I wanted to talk to you personally. I have some questions about how this year isn't going to be the same shit as last year," he said, as I started wishing my principal had told me about this guy, "and I've been reading some stuff online that makes me very worried about how you'll treat my son."

Oh god.

So we sat down. His manila folder was full of essays and articles

I had written online, as well as the comment sections, highlighted, to some of those essays. I swear more than infrequently in my writing. I figured this was the issue he had, but no. This wasn't that.

His primary worry was that, and don't get him wrong here, social justice and all that stuff is important, and he's the very last person in the world who would be racist and in fact he went to school mostly with Blacks, but doing all this constant social justice stuff in class, talking about how white people did this and white people did that, and, I mean, there were good white people, too, who fought in the civil war to free the slaves, and also don't even get him started on all this gender-pronoun stuff, I mean, why can't kids just say their names instead of being made to feel attacked, and anyway . . . . Here's the big worry: he was worried that if we talked about racism in school, it would make his son feel uncomfortable to the point that his son would become a Nazi.

"I mean, this is how you get school shooters," he said.

I've dealt with upset parents before. Very often they are upset for good reason, or because sometimes stories from school go home experienced and remembered and translated in the brain of a thirteen-year-old and there are some misconceptions that need to be cleared up. This was my first time dealing with a parent upset before I'd ever laid eyes on their kid, though, and this guy was averaging three things a sentence that I really wanted to argue with him about, which, I bet, is what he wanted more than anything.

I really *really* tried my best to both diffuse the situation and be completely honest. My first step was to tell myself, over and over in my head, "It's not your job to fix this man." My work is with kids, with eighth graders, and not with the sociopolitical beliefs of their parents.

So I said this . . . or, rather, I tried to say this but got interrupted every ten seconds or so with more invitations to argue that I declined in order to stay on point (I won't write all those in, but you can imagine them if you'd like): "I need you to understand, first, that the writing I do online is who I am, for sure, but not always what I will be like in class with your student. My main work, the work I really care most about in the world, is my classroom, and I can't do that work well if my students feel attacked or marginalized or silenced by me. So I need you to give me a chance, know that I will never intentionally try to teach students what to think, but will work hard all year to give them tools about how to think critically and how to listen and understand each other. If there's any point that your son feels I have made him uncomfortable or unsafe, and he tells you, tell me right away and I will make it better. Until then, I don't think it's helpful to argue about what we think might happen. Instead, let's work together to make your son's eighth grade year better than last year, and, you know, as good as it can possibly be."

And then he kissed me.

He didn't.

But we shook hands and he left a little less certain that I was the social justice maniac he thought I was. And somewhere in talking with him, there in my mostly empty classroom, I had finally put words to my plan for the year.

SEPTEMBER

THE YEAR STARTS

IN MY VERY FIRST CLASS ON MY FIRST day I had a kid who was, even as an eighth grader, bigger and taller than I am by far. He was wearing a football jersey that stretched tightly across his back as if they somehow don't make football jerseys his size. That first day he was carrying a full gallon jug of water around with him into classes. When I asked about it, he told me he used the jug not for its potential hydration capabilities but for the utility of its weight. "I don't drink it. It's just heavy." He was allowed to carry a water bottle around, he said, and this was his. He used it to work out in class, lifting it above and then behind his head, three sets of twenty reps. Each arm, of course.

I remember wondering, for the first (but not the last) time, as I watched him count his reps, just what in the hell I was doing in the suburbs.

In my class I start with personal identity stuff. We do this activity, shamelessly stolen and adapted from some training thing years ago, where students write five words that describe their identity—who they are, what they are like, where they are from. I do this along with them as a way to share about myself as we are first starting to get to know one another. I've done the activity every year for about a decade now, and my five words change here and there but are generally these: dad, teacher, writer, anxious, antiracist (I say "social justice warrior" if I'm in the mood to try to be funny).

It does not escape me that even after all this work I've done over the past many years digging into my own racial identity and history, studying systemic racism and privilege, that I still don't list my race, gender, or sexuality on there, though most people whose identities are often screwed over by people who share my identities will. So, yes, it's hugely important, I know that it is, that I am white and straight and a cisgender guy and able bodied and college educated and financially secure. That isn't just a list of all the things I know I'm supposed to say, seriously. Each and every one of those things is a huge part of my daily life, but I don't write any of those things down as one of my top five.

The very first time I did this activity, this guy I worked with whom I didn't (don't) like at all got in a whole argument with the presenter because he couldn't think of any other words other than *white* and *male,* so all-consuming was his desire to talk about his whiteness and maleness, like an *SNL* skit about a wokest white dude. I never want to be that guy, so I try to avoid having the "right" answer and instead try to be honest and then reflect on what my honesty means about me.

Anyway, once the whole class and I have our five things, we slowly cross them off one at a time with discussions about what we picked and why. I drop the "dad" at some point, which is hard, but I explain that I do so because though it's the most important thing I do, it really only impacts my immediate family. The discussions give us a way to talk about race and culture and family, they touch on individual and cultural identity, and since everyone is only talking about themselves, it is generally comfortable and safe.

When we have our last word, the students all make a deco-rated little rectangle sheet of it and hang them on the back wall. They are the first things up in my room every year, and that first year there included the words *Tibetan, Creative, Brother, Activist*; four girls who all wrote *Black* and hung them all together; about fifteen kids who wrote *Gamer*; and though I warn them over and over again to double-check, there are a whole lot of misspellings of single words (including an *Atlete* and two *Cristains*). At its best, the activity works as a way for students to put a piece of themselves up in my room. It's a nice first step on a very long path. The football weightlifting kid? His word was *history*. Huh.

No matter what I do in my teaching, I have learned, again and again, that recognizing and affirming the identities of my students needs to come first and needs to be my constant work.

The phrase *cultural competency* gets used a lot, but in my head it's a word I would use to describe a specific culture that I have learned a lot about. I don't try to teach my students competency about a single culture. Instead, my goal is something more like cultural literacy. I want them to have the skills to see and appreciate differences in culture, to recognize their own, to know where and how to get information when they have questions, to read what parts of a given conflict or misunderstanding may be personal and which may be cultural.

Because also, here's the thing: kids talk about super challenging stuff whether we ask them to or not. When parents came to me early in the year to ask why we were talking about "race stuff" and not "regular English stuff," I had a long answer ready for how social context serves skills content, but also a real answer about how kids need tools to explore and question and discuss difficult ideas without hurting one another, to have discussions productively instead of destructively. So I do my best to give them those tools and try to let them take it from there.

That's a lot, but, honestly, the groups of kids I see in my room now are far, far better at cultural literacy than any other group of people I've encountered in my life. This group of kids has grown up on the internet, has grown up with constant access to different people, different ideas, different modes of expression.

Ollie once came into my classroom and glanced at my book-shelves. They asked, "Do you have students at your school that speak other languages?"

"Yes."

"Then why don't you have books in other languages?"

"Because . . ." Damn. I hadn't really even thought of it, but my daughter was on it. Instantly. That kind of cultural literacy is something they will need in the world, and, as a white person, something the world needs them to have.

A good portion of my class, then, involves giving vocabulary and frameworks to things they already understand, and perhaps helping them apply those things in new ways. On many days, or even most, I wouldn't say that I am leading an antiracist classroom. My best hope is that I am helping to facilitate one, to give room for that kind of work without trying to force it to look or sound a particular way.

Race is always on the table, and we work hard at the beginning of the year to make the room a safe place to talk and ask questions about race and any number of other challenging subjects. I follow the students' lead about when and how those conversations happen. There are a few times that I'm teaching something, like the stages of genocide, or redlining as an example of systemic racism (on this day, later in the year, I tell the story of my grandpas). There are frameworks and statistics and history our kids should know, but I think of antiracism more as a skill, as a set of skills rather than a set of knowledge. As a white guy, there was a lot of work for me between understanding that racist stuff is bad and understanding how to look for it, name it, be able to explain how it is operating in a given situation, and begin to deconstruct the supports around it. Getting there takes practice that is deeper and more consistent than the right posters on the wall or the right novels on the shelf.

I've spent the better part of fifteen years trying to learn how to teach through an antiracist lens. When I started teaching, I was most interested in teaching young artists about writing and art stuff. I still love that part of my work, but I have stayed passionate about teaching, stayed angry and exhausted and hopeful about teaching, because of the opportunities I see there to impact racism in a meaningful way. So we work to understand how our identities impact our perceptions, and how our histories have shaped our present.

Antiracism is firmly tied to my identity as a teacher. I'm not perfect or great or sometimes even good at doing it, but I know I am at least trying to do that work every day. As a dad, though, I know I've got a lot more I could be doing.

I'm raising a white kid, and I do my best to think about that a lot, but Ollie and I haven't talked about it as much as we could or should.

By and large, white people don't find it particularly easy to talk about race. That much, I think, most people would agree on, but the reality of it is a bit more complicated. Really, once we spend some time breaking past all the original discomfort and unlearning some of the color-blindness stuff we learned from very special episodes of '80s sitcoms, we get pretty good at talking about how bad racism is. White teachers especially can get a little too comfortable talking about how bad racism is and can find themselves suddenly trying to teach classrooms of kids of color about how much they totally get now, or just focusing on the awfulness of all the awful to the point that we stop expecting our kids of color to do much in class. Surely, it's okay if they never read the book or whatever, because of all the racisms, right?

Our ease in talking about some of the worst parts of racism makes some sense. These things give us a chance to perform anger or sadness or understanding, especially if there's a person of color who may notice.

What we white people really hate doing is talking about white people. Many of us have grown up with a developed understanding that racism is something that happens to other people, that, really, race is something that other people have.

I helped lead a meeting of our staff last year. Our equity team was trying to set some shared understanding of the culture of our building and how it may have been structured and supported by our staff. So, like in my own classroom, we started with personal identity, and though I have seen this assumption proved wrong a thousand different ways, I figured I could skip past the real beginner stuff, because adults would be better at talking about race.

It turns out that when you ask white adults to talk about their own racial histories, you'll hear a whole lot of stories about their first Black friend. We address race by talking about our proximity to people of color. It's easier to talk about this bad thing that happened to our friend or partner or kid or colleague who is a person of color than it is to talk about the good things that have happened to us because of our whiteness. In other words, we use people of color as shields from really thinking about our own role. I tried very hard to get all my white colleagues to not do that. Also, when I think about raising Olive to understand race and privilege, I end up thinking a lot about how they have some friends who aren't white, so I must be doing just fine. It's a bullshit reason not to do the work. I know that for the adults but still use it with my own kid because this is all pretty messy and difficult.

Becca and I got really lucky, though. We have a kid who asks a ton of questions, who always wants to understand how the world works, and who is empathetic to the point of absurdity. They've also gone to day cares and schools that were racially diverse and that celebrated (rather than pretended not to see) the diversity among their student bodies. Ollie's favorite teacher ever, their second grade teacher, was a Somali and Muslim woman. (This is especially not typical of the usual Minnesota school experience, a state where something like 97.5 percent of all teachers are white.) In addition to all that, Ollie just is, and always has been, committed to justice, to righting whatever wrongs they can. When they were very young, like four or five, an aunt came up to them at a Christmas party. The kids had all gotten little bubble machine things in different colors, and Ollie had gotten a blue one. The aunt said, "Let me go find you one that isn't a boy color." She was trying to helpful, but good god, did Ollie let her have it, not gently, quietly, or quickly explaining to the aunt that there are no such things as boy or girl colors or toys or clothes. Ollie continued this monologue on the car ride back from the party: "And what if a boy got a pink one and someone said that was a girl color, but he actually really liked that color?"

A few years later, after hearing kids in their class at the old school who were scared about new anti-immigration laws and rhetoric, Ollie had a weekend-long lemonade stand that raised like $400 for pro-immigrant sources. And when some recently immigrated students were being bullied in their home language (which teachers didn't speak or understand), Ollie spoke up during a classroom discussion with a statement that ended up getting spread around the school until a fourth grade class adopted it and made it into a giant banner that hung about the office. It said, "Kids that speak another language are like super heroes. We expect them to do good with their powers," which, like, I have notes or whatever on some of the wording there, but they were in second grade and hadn't fully internalized Twitter activism yet.

Anyway, it came as no surprise to us that three days into third grade Ollie was already shaking things up at their new school. This was before Ollie had officially started using they/them pronouns, but they were increasingly upset at how often gender was being used to divide kids during the day. *Boys* and *Girls* were used to form lunch lines, to dismiss classes, to set groups for activities, to move from recess, for a bunch of little things all throughout the day. It's the kind of thing everyone was doing without really thinking about it, which I no doubt have done in my own class-room without thinking about it, but that made Olive uncomfort-able over and over and over again.

Ollie's never really been one to hang out in discomfort, though, and Ollie is a pretty big badass. After a gym class where boys and girls were broken up repeatedly for various lines and groups, Ollie saw the principal in the hallway. They went right up to him and asked if he had time to talk. Ollie explained to him how the divid-ing by gender was making them uncomfortable, and that probably there were other kids in the school who felt the same.

That day, when I picked Ollie up from school, the principal no-ticed us outside. He came over, introduced himself to me, told me a bit about what happened, and then dropped to a knee (this is the moment I decided I really liked their principal, since he wanted to have the conversation with Ollie, not me) to update Ollie. He told them that things would be changing from here on out, that Ollie was completely right, and that no kid should be made to feel un-comfortable at school. He also showed that he'd been really think-ing about it by sharing a list of things (birth month, shoe color, first letters of names) that could be used to divide kids quickly without relying on gender. He'd be talking to all the teachers, he said, and wanted to know from Ollie if it happened again.

See? Ollie's a badass.

If the principal was hoping that listening to and addressing Ollie's concerns would help them feel more empowered and com-fortable at school, he did a great job. If he was hoping that solving this one problem would make Ollie relax and quit stirring things up, he was desperately wrong.

Over the course of just the first few months, Ollie started a few different petitions in the school. One was to start a school newspaper, another was to offer a Meatless Monday vegetarian entree once a week in the school cafeteria (Ollie was, at that point, not vegetarian, and also does not eat school lunch). Ollie seemed to be meeting with the principal every couple of weeks about one thing or another that they were working on, and I couldn't have been happier, though I did notice that where their dad couldn't stop talking about race, Ollie had become focused on gender identity and expression.

OCTOBER

THE INFAMOUS C-WORD CONFERENCE

THE FIRST CONFERENCE AT OLLIE'S NEW school has gone down in family history for two reasons. Primarily, it is remembered as the school conference where Becca swore. She didn't mean to, or, rather, didn't even know she was swearing. She said something off-handed about everything that comes home in folders that we sometimes (nearly always) forget to look through. Ollie looked at me and I looked at Ollie and we both looked at the teacher and the teacher looked at Becca. All of us understood, except Becca, that in third grade classrooms, even when it's dark outside, you're not supposed to say *crap*.

Ollie played it cool until we were in the car on the way home, after congratulations were given for a solid report from their teacher about Ollie trying hard and catching up quickly to the kids who had been in the program for years, and there was a lull in conversation as we hit the highway home.

"Uhh, Mom. You swore," came the voice from the back, about 80 percent amused and 20 percent horrified.

"What? I did not."

"Yeah, you did," Ollie and I said in unison.

"No, I didn't!" Becca's one of those people who will look over both shoulders before talking about someone who lives four states

65

away, who is always afraid of embarrassing herself. (She once called after one of my professors who came to our house for dinner, "Thanks for coming on me!" and still gets upset if that professor is mentioned in our home.) She's also a sex therapist and educator who uses words and discusses concepts all day that sometimes sneak around the edges of other conversations (like when she yelled after one of my professors). So she's always worried that she's said something wrong.

"You said the C-word," I tried to explain.

"I did *not,*" she said, obviously scanning her memory to see what she could have said that sounded like *that* C-word.

"You said *crap.*"

"Dad!" (from the back).

Becca protested. "That's not a swear word!"

"Yes, it is!" said Ollie and I, again, in unison. (We are a dangerous pair when our brains line up like this, which is kind of often.) We were all shouting now, through the laughter, because our family gets a tremendous kick out of itself.

"It's a swear word in third grade," I explained, "and you totally got a look from the teacher."

"No . . ."

"Yep," Ollie piped in again. "She looked at you like you're in trouble."

So it's now become shorthand in our house, used almost exclusively by Olive, who is the only one who cares about swearing. When someone swears, especially when they use the C-word, Ollie will shout from just about anywhere in the house, car, or public event where we are, "Teacher conference!"

So that's the main reason we'll remember that conference forever.

The secondary reason, just no big deal, is that it's the first time Ollie told us they were nonbinary. Their teacher was saying something (no doubt something hugely glowing like, "Wow, she must have the best dad in the entire world," obviously), and Ollie interrupted, "Umm . . . excuse me? You said 'she'? And I use they/them pronouns."

Which is cool and awesome, and I'm glad Ollie was so comfortable correcting their teacher, and also Ollie had never told anyone that ever, so we did have to explain that, you know, people aren't likely to just guess that you have different pronouns from what have been used for you for the past eight years.

Really, though, it wasn't a big surprise.

For about a year Ollie had been saying things like, "I don't really feel like a boy or a girl, I just feel like an Ollie." And, sure, we were really hoping Ollie would settle on an identity outside cisgender and heterosexual, because it would give both me and Becca extra social-justice-y points in our various professions, but we also didn't try to rush them toward anything or make a big deal about it.

It would be nice to say that once we were told, we only ever saw Ollie as nonbinary, only ever used their correct pronouns—such was the strength of the joint powers of our own understanding about the construction of gender and our commitment to our child. It would even be nice to say that still, years later, we don't (especially me) still accidentally use *she* or *her* when referring to Olive. It's hard, it really is. Since the first moment I held (and nearly passed out and dropped) this new being in the world, they'd been a girl, and though we deemphasized gendered toys and clothes, they liked to wear dresses and had dolls and played more dress-up than football. No matter how much we know those things don't define gender, how much some of that could have been Ollie playing to expectations, they were a girl, in our minds and in our language, and adapting to new language, a new way of seeing them, took time and practice.

It really helped to practice, to make sure we corrected each other even when Ollie wasn't around, to steer sentences toward using pronouns instead of away. Eventually, maybe months for me, I started using the right pronouns for Ollie, even when just thinking about them, and started saying them without the pause to mentally translate old pronouns to new, started to feel that *she* and *her* sounded clunky and incorrect.

A few months after Ollie announced they were nonbinary, I was on a walk with one of my aunts while we were down visiting family in Wisconsin. (You may hear a lot about aunts in this book. Between Becca's family and mine, there are fourteen aunts. So I have lots of aunts, and also, since there are enough of them to allow for some anonymity, *aunt* makes a good stand-in for *family member I'd rather not name specifically*). She'd been trying all weekend during the visit to use they/them but missed as often as she hit. On the walk, she told me about not always feeling like a really girlie girl herself growing up and so was understanding a bit through that lens. She also voiced some concern that maybe that's what was going on with Ollie, and she hoped Ollie understood that you can be a girl and still not like pink stuff and dolls. There was a worry, I think, that Ollie may grow up and feel different and also feel stuck in a decision they made when they were eight.

I've made sure Ollie knows that I am as worried about them deciding some permanent gender identity right now as I am about them picking their college major before they get to fifth grade. Ollie could identify as nonbinary for the rest of their life, or could identify as male or female, or have an identity that fluidly runs across the spectrum. As far as Becca and I are concerned, Ollie never ever needs to decide.

My mom voiced similar concerns at first, and though she never used the word *phase*, I could understand why she may be concerned. This is the woman who lived through my high school freshman phase when I declared myself a Young Republican, and then my high school sophomore phase when I identified as a Communist, bought a cool CCCP T-shirt, and read like half of the *Communist Manifesto* (in that order).

A year later, I was a Buddhist poet, born decades late for the Beat Generation but convinced I was somehow still a member. By my senior year of high school, I was dying my hair pink, wearing tights on my arms, leather and spike bracelets, and silver glitter eyeliner on my face, dressing up every day like I was going to a white rebellion in the suburbs–themed party (not a bad idea for a party).

Even though she lived through all that, it didn't take my mom long to do with Ollie what she had spent a very successful career as a special education teacher doing: listening to and trusting young people. Ollie has not wavered in their identity in the past year, and though Ollie has been very patient with people misgendering them, it's obvious how it wears on them when it's too much for too long. There was one long camping weekend with both sets of grandparents and assorted cousins and siblings and whatnot. It was a fun weekend of camping and adventures, and also a weekend of a whole lot of people who had known for months and months that Ollie was nonbinary, most of whom were in their own process of growth and struggle and who were really working at it, and some who had seemed to have decided to just stop trying.

During one quieter moment, Ollie pulled me aside and asked if I would remind a few aunts we were with (so many aunts, right?). While we talked about it, Ollie explained just how complicated it was. They said they always noticed when someone used the wrong pronoun, but that it didn't always bother them, but when it did bother them, they didn't always want to stop the whole conversation or whatever just to point it out, or didn't want them to feel bad, or didn't want to draw a bunch of attention to themselves about it. It's a sentiment, I am sure, many people feel often about the daily stabs of discomfort or dismissal they feel when any part of their identity does not conform to whatever the hell "normal" is supposed to be.

In general, we've been awfully lucky at how well Ollie's family and school community have worked to support them. After that long camping weekend, and after one of those hard-sleeping nights you have after a long weekend camping, I woke up to a text from my mom:

> *For Ollie*
> *There was a little girl*
> *Who had a few curls wearing beads, bangles, and bells.*
>
> *When she grew a little older*
> *She grew a little bolder*
> *With her thoughts, actions, and art.*
>
> *Now they are such a treasure*
> *They show us to follow our pleasure*
> *We love them and all they are.*

The poem was followed by a message: "We love you, Ollie. I may not always remember to say they and them, but my mind knows who you are and how you feel. I try to show that by finding clothes that are comfortable for you."

True. Ever since Ollie was born, my mom would bring a suitcase of thrift store finds for them when she came to visit. Until a very recent move, we had a small pile of abandoned thrift store suitcases in our basement as proof. (This is how my mom travels: rather than buying expensive stuff to carry around, she buys stuff at thrift stores to get her where she's going and donates as she goes. It's brilliant.) As Ollie's tastes have changed, my mom has been very adept at changing her finds right with them. Frilly big dress things and unicorns have been replaced with a tight rotation of jeans, tank tops, and hoodies. A solid 60 percent of Ollie's wardrobe comes from my mom, and I hadn't paused to think of it yet as an act of love until she sent that message. Now it's hard to miss.

We do our best to give Ollie positive reinforcement like my mom's poem, and to make sure they are spending time around people across the LGBTQIA spectrum, people Ollie doesn't have to explain or defend themselves to, because in so much of Ollie's time and space that we can't control, it's far too often they have to do both. This was especially true during the first few months of their new school year in their new school with all their new classmates.

We are working hard to do the right thing with Olive and their gender. I'm sure we're making mistakes, but we do our best to let Ollie know they are supported and loved and appreciated, and that we respect who they are and how they identify. At the same time, we also don't want to push or lead the way. When Ollie told us that they didn't feel totally like a boy or a girl, we did not say, "You are nonbinary! Let's go watch YouTube videos about it!" We let them decide, gave them information when they asked. It turned out that they had watched all the YouTube videos anyway and knew all the history and slang and flag colors and a fair amount of pretty advanced gender theory.

When we send Ollie off to school, we're not always sure how it will be. There is a friend who refuses to stop using *she,* who has told Ollie directly that they don't "believe" in nonbinary people. I mostly let Ollie navigate that, while letting them know I'm willing to go fight that third grader as soon as asked. Ollie's annoyed by the misgendering but has decided for now to let it slide.

At the same time, Ollie's making waves at the school. Since

Ollie has started identifying at school as nonbinary, two other kids in their class have felt comfortable enough to do so as well. They have a little friend group of eight-year-old kids with undercuts, and it's pretty much the cutest ever. Halfway through that first semester there, we went in for a curriculum night, the kind of thing where you go around and experience different aspects of your students' school day and see whatever project they are working on and mostly just try not to make your face look like you'd rather be anywhere else in the world.

While there, Becca and I were approached by other parents. Their second grader had spent the past year feeling uncomfortable at school because they too were nonbinary. They had told a few people but didn't feel like their decision was being fully honored or recognized. Usually the teacher would use they/them pronouns but wouldn't step in when kids were misgendering or challenging that kid's identity. That sort of hands-off approach sent a message to the whole class that this pronoun switch wasn't a real thing, and the kid retreated. A different local district spent years pushing the "neutral" response to any gender or sexuality issues, and the result was story after story of horrific bullying gone unchecked and a string of student suicides. Silence isn't neutral.

I don't think Ollie's school before had any schoolwide policy or established culture around gender, which means things depended broadly on the kids around you and the adults in the room. Then came Olive, loud as can be and a year older (a BIG kid!), and Ollie pushing on the school, and the school reacting with some much-needed discussions among staff and with students about gender identity.

The parents came up to us to express their thanks. Not to us, of course, but to Ollie, whose very presence in the school had meant so much to their kid, though the two rarely ever talked.

It's not hard to be super proud of my kid.

It gives me pause, really, the power and empathy and energy for justice young people show. I've been teaching a pretty decently long amount of time and am no stranger to the kinds of struggles and successes and awkwardnesses that teenage people face. That said, in my first year of teaching eighth grade, I had exactly zero students that I know of who were transitioning genders or had transitioned or who identified as nonbinary. I don't think there were any the next year or the next year either. There are students who have since come out, once they hit the mostly adult-ish world of college, but nothing about them as eighth graders suggested to me they were unhappy or incomplete with that part of themselves.

This year of teaching, fourteen years after my first, I have two students who have transitioned (that I know of), and four students in some process of figuring that out. Ollie is in fourth grade and wears a backpack to school every day with a cartoon picture of cats stacked on top of each other, each a different color in a way that represents the nonbinary pride flag (another gift from my mom). When they got to their school last year, they were the only openly nonbinary kid there. Now there are five or so. To the eyes of a terrified transphobe, I'm sure the only logical conclusion is that "this gender stuff" is spreading, that these kids are being convinced that they are confused, and that some great disservice is being done. From what I've seen, anyway, people don't come out in college because that's when the gay kicks in. People come out when they can, when they're comfortable, or when the damage of staying closeted outweighs the risk of coming out.

I may not understand any of it fully, having been born in a body I feel comfortable in. (I mean, I'm deeply deeply uncomfortable in it, but not for any reasons related to gender.) I may never fully understand what it is to feel otherwise. But then, here's the great thing: I don't ever need to. I just need to listen to the innumerable voices out there that have, are, or will transition and believe what they tell me.

There are those who feel like young people shouldn't be talking about gender, or learning to understand and accept everyone around them. I don't feel that way. Even more important than how I feel, Ollie doesn't feel that way. The eighth graders I work with don't feel that way. In fact, many of them feel like they have waited much longer than was comfortable to finally be who they are, who would have loved to have waited until they were out of their home but just couldn't.

I often think of this one kid, Edward, whom I taught during his sophomore year of high school, a few schools ago now. We were doing this thing in class one day. It was the Friday of a week that had been a few months long, most of it spent on the Stages of Genocide and how they related to an oppressed group of each student's choosing. It had been a heavy, heavy week in class. So Friday I gave us a bit of a break to read something fun online.

We read this cool little thing about how we generally have a hundred ten-minute blocks in our waking day. Following the suggestion of the piece ("100 Blocks a Day" by Tim Urban) students filled out a hundred-square grid with how they had spent the previous day ("What if I don't remember yesterday, like, at all?" asked more than one student) and then another grid for a day they would consider ideal. Try as I might to have them take the activity seriously, there was a lot of talk of wearing wedding dresses bowling, of dates with members of the US Women's Soccer team, of naps followed by naps capped off with going to bed five hours early (again, it had been a long week). Silly though many of them were, they were still really fun to hear about, and I was rather enjoying my Friday full of goofy kids with goofy plans.

Then I got to Edward. Edward who is, without rival, the funniest kid in the grade, who finishes every assignment two days early and three feet deeper than anyone else, who is nearly always smiling, joking, being ridiculous. I walked by Ed's group as he was starting to share his ideal day.

"Okay, so I wake up, and my dad accepts me"—this step took up two squares. Twenty minutes of being accepted, "then I get top surgery, and after that I eat mac & cheese and go to bed." Ed is like this, funny and heartbreaking and strong and vulnerable all at once and all the time.

He had transitioned the year before, and friends embraced and celebrated it, and the school tried to be not shitty about it and mostly succeeded (though still struggled to offer places to change for gym or pee comfortably). Ed will write a book of his own someday, hopefully sooner than later, so I won't try to tell his story here.

I will say that I heard there was friction with him at home last year, and in a moment when Ed was working alone, I sat next to him and asked him if, whenever I needed to have contact with parents, he had preferences about how to handle that.

"You should dead-name me," he said. For those who don't know, *dead-naming* is when a person who has transitioned genders is referred to by their old name. It's a shitty thing to do, a thing that erases that person's true self, that tells them you don't believe them when they tell you who they are, often something that brings up a lot of trauma and pain from a hard time in their life. Here, Edward was telling me to dead-name him to his parents. "Every time my dad hears anyone call me Edward, I just get lectured to anyway."

My first interaction with Edward's dad happened a few months into the year. His email was interesting, to say the least, mixing the tone and language of someone with one foot still planted firmly in the '60s, referring to chunks of my curriculum as "very groovy stuff," but also telling me my interest in hip-hop was an obvious ploy to seem cool to kids that wasn't fooling anyone. I looked him up on Facebook, as I often do before I respond to an email from someone I don't know well. There he was, the haircut of Patrick Swayze in *Road House* and a rugby jersey fitting him exactly as well as any of my high school clothes would fit me right now. So I had information, but no pieces of the puzzle that really fit yet.

Things can't be easy for young Edward, though you'd never know when first meeting him. His confidence and charm are overwhelming, as is his penchant for being wildly inappropriate. He always seemed most happy when getting to ask any number of professional guests, visiting principals or artists or speakers, what their favorite felony is, and by way of a follow-up explaining that his goal is to be the first trans man in a male federal prison.

His first project of the year was a painting of an astronaut in a space suit against a field of stars. The astronaut held a sign that said, "I'm too gay for this." It will hang on the wall of every classroom I have forever. One day I had students find the most interesting fact they could, to share with the class. Edwards was "Every potato is unique."

He is one of the funniest and smartest people I've ever had in my classroom. He had a group of friends who cared deeply for him when he wasn't annoying the shit out of them. He had a school that in most ways and in most places accepted him, but, also, his name wasn't Edward in our attendance program, which means every time he logged into a school computer or got a school email or took a standardized test, or a substitute teacher read a roster that a teacher forgot to adapt, he had to use a name that isn't his. The school needs parent permission to change the name of record.

I wrote an email to Edward's dad once. I let him know it wasn't my place to do so, that I wasn't writing in my capacity as an English teacher, but just guy to guy. I told him he had a great kid, a kid who wants to and should work for NASA someday, told a quick story or two about something great Edward had done without using his name or a pronoun, trying to ease my way in. This was just after Olive was born, and I told him I imagined it was hard, you know, when the kid you've known as a girl every day of their life tells you they aren't. I told him if he ever wanted to talk about it, dad to dad, I'd be open to it.

He never wrote back.

I worry about Edward pretty regularly. The rate of suicide among transgender teens is horrific. It isn't my place to tell the parents of my students how to parent their child, but I'm so fucking angry at any parent who can't, won't, or doesn't support their transgender kid. Like, even if you think it's fake (it's not) and even if you think it's a phase (probably isn't) and even if it's confusing to you and you don't like it, I ask this question of you: so fucking what?

If you're right and being transgender is a mind-control prank caused by Liberal radio waves and fluoride, and it just happens to be documented through the whole history of us, what do you lose by calling your kid the name they want to be called? What does it cost you to use the pronouns they are most comfortable with? Not as much, not nearly as much, as it could cost to raise a child in a house that they know doesn't fully accept them.

Ollie knows what houses on the way home from school have pride flags. They notice when people, when anyone at all, uses or asks for pronouns before assuming. They know who stubbornly keeps using the wrong pronouns for them and who embraces their identity. A lot of this is tough, a lot of this is going to keep being tough. There's some deep work that needs to be done, there's some real, meaningful support Ollie is going to need. But from everyone who can give it, even just the surface stuff can feel really *really* important.

NOVEMBER

ART AND WEIRDOS

THE SECOND-BEST EVENT OF OLLIE'S third grade year was the music concert. It was amazing because one of Ollie's friends had made a giant (as in, wearable) cardboard submarine for their Valentine's Day box competition (which is apparently a thing now), and the teacher had the last-minute idea to have the kid walk on wearing it while the class sang "Yellow Submarine." The cardboard boat was painted blue. On his way across the stage, trying to weave and turn like a submarine, the kid knocked over three different microphones while everyone onstage tried to sing through laughter (except Olive, who was openly guffawing). It was the best. Well, the second-best.

The actual best event of the school year fell right in the middle of the nonsense festival that happens in the weeks between Thanksgiving and winter break. Every kind of graduation or awards ceremony or academic-showcase-something pales in comparison. Even the music concert does not hold a candle to the late-late-fall gathering for the school talent show.

That year's show featured every school's consistent lineup of solo kids singing Disney songs (sometimes the same song, or maybe they all just sound like the same song). There were also a few acts of dance choreography with two friends who were super into it and one friend waiting for it to be over. Pretty standard stuff. But Ollie's new school also had three magic shows, two of which were done by different kids both named Bjorn. Another kid did "T.N.T." by AC/DC on his bass, and yet another did a karate demonstration with his mom (complete with bad-guy costumes!). I mean, honestly, they should televise this thing.

Ollie had no doubt that they were going to perform in the talent show, signing up before they had come up with an idea. By the time the show rolled around, they had a whole routine down. The program said "Speed Drawing" by Ollie's name, but really it was *improvised* speed drawing. Ollie came out, did a little patter with the crowd, growing about three inches taller with every laugh they got, then asked for a suggestion for a thing to draw. Once they got the suggestion, they did a little prearranged hand signal and the *Jeopardy* theme music started, signaling that Ollie had thirty seconds to draw that thing. They scrambled down to their pad, drawing away until the bell sounded, and showed their drawing to the crowd. The crowd member (not planted) had suggested Ollie draw a cat. Ollie always draws cats, so they really really nailed this one.

I loved it for so many reasons, but most of all because Ollie wanted to perform and though they can sing and act and play instruments, the thing they care most about is their drawing, so they figured out a way to perform a generally not-performance art. More and more, art is not just something that Ollie does, and being an artist is something they are, something that has shifted the way they see and interact with the world even when they aren't drawing. I went through that, too, once upon a time, as a writer, though it took me more years than Ollie to get to it.

When I was fifteen, I was pretty sure I was America's best living poet. This was in the age before the internet was actually the internet. As far as my school library and English classes taught me, there were no other living poets. So I won not only by my uncontainable genius, but also by default. It was a win I was willing to embrace.

Like all world's best poets, I had been trying kinda hard for almost two whole years. I spent most of middle school reading one book, just one, *Jurassic Park,* over and over again every night. Then one night, before lying down, my brain demanded something else from me. It said I should write down a bunch of feelings and images and stuff on a piece of paper, just because. I was, remember, an eighth grader. My brain was almost always telling me things I didn't understand. But also because I was an eighth grader, I never seemed to question the things my brain would ask of me.

I wrote a poem. It was at least a year before I would put that name to that thing. Thirteen years old or so, and I had no real idea what a poem was. Instead, I carried around some suspicion that I had in fact invented a thing.

I wrote the thing, folded it about a million times, and hid it on a shelf in my room. Occasionally, I would take it out and read it, but more often I would just take it out to look at it, outside of the folds. It was this secret and powerful thing I had done, and I had no idea why. At some point I lost it, because things like that get lost eventually. It's probably for the best, because now I can remember it fondly as something wonderful.

So I had written but was not yet officially a writer. That moment did not happen until the summer after my freshman year of high school. I signed up to go to an art camp, because I had done some theater and occasionally drew funny pictures of cows and stuff, and because, I think, my parents had started to get worried about me. When I registered, I neglected to sign up for a primary art, the one thing I would be studying and working on every day, so the camp people took me around to all the different classes and had me choose one. Theater looked good, and the art class was held in the sculpture room and had these floor-to-ceiling shelves full of every random thing in the world and could hardly have been more appealing. But in the end I chose writing. It was a life-altering moment, very likely the reason this book even exists, and it happened because in the writing class I was going to be the only boy.

That week transformed me. I was a writer. It was who I was. It was this badge on my chest, and I was sure everyone could see it. By the end of the week, one girl from my class called my dorm room, invited me to sneak down to hers to make out, and I told her no. I was working on a poem. By the next day, she was holding hands with someone else, and I was okay with that, mostly. Poetry was powerful and dangerous, after all, but girls were terrifying.

That experience, at ArtsWorld in Steven's Point, Wisconsin, is probably in the top-three most important things in my life. The first two are partnering with Becca and having Olive, so, you know, big things. That the third thing is two weeks, one in 1997, the other a year later, I spent at an arts camp in the middle of Wisconsin doesn't really make sense. The stuff I wrote there is forever lost, and I don't really remember what happened in the classes at all. I know it is where I learned that art was important to me, that young people make art that is beautiful even when it's awful, that I was a writer.

Since then, I have always written. Always. I wrote poetry through high school and remember one particularly awful four-page rhyming poem about a proposal, "a box burning a hole in my pocket, for her. All proposals before, shallow they were." Ugh. This was around that time that I thought I was probably the best in the world. (You know. Obviously.) I also remember climbing into the back-back seat of my family's Toyota minivan and my brother telling me, gently, that a lot of writers try to focus on the things they actually know about and have experienced. I mean . . . what did he know?

At ArtsWorld, I met kids who were like me. Kids who were

weird and obsessed with big weird ideas, who liked making stuff and performing, and who were, almost to a kid, outcasts in whatever Wisconsin town they were from. It was that experience, more than probably any other thing about the camp, that was important to me. Meeting other artsy kids gave me permission to accept who I was, how I thought, what I cared about.

The first summer, there were equal parts inspiration and trepidation. By the second year I was out of my goddamn mind with confidence in my mediocre-ass self. I wrote short poems that didn't make sense AND used incorrect grammar because I never paid attention to the grammar stuff in class. I made a huge poster that said, "Like fish / Than Drowning" and should have used "then" (but it's dumb either way). The theater building, where we had our classes, had one of those vending machines that sold half tuna sandwiches and yogurt and stuff. I bought a ton of them out and replaced the food inside with pieces of scrap metal from the sculpture room with fake-deep things written on them like "Art is Murder."

I was a lot.

When I got to college, I stumbled into an Introduction to Poetry class with Michael Dennis Browne. He's a brilliant and terrifying man, one who taught me as much about the power and beauty in teaching as in writing. He also gently but firmly disabused me of my belief that I had done anything interesting to that point with my writing. He was one of two poles of art and writing in my undergrad years.

The other was a group of musicians I met in the dorms and then lived with in an apartment that probably still smells like our unwashed dishes. They were rappers and producers in the local hip-hop scene, and I was the weird poet kid who hung out with them that no one cared about. This meant that evenings were often spent at stuffy poetry reading things where all the women wore big scarfs tied fifty times around their necks and the men all had neatly trimmed white beards and untamed bushes of nose hair. After, I would sometimes find my way to something cool like some dark concert venue or illegal warehouse show, but most often I would tag along to something called a "listening party," where a bunch of hip-hop heads would sit around and listen to the entirety of someone's new album, chain-smoking cigarettes and declaring everything they heard "dope." It's a toss-up as to which thing I pretended to like most.

In the meantime I wrote a bunch of poems. Some of them started to get pretty good. My first paid gig was reading poems at a monthly series that paid each performer forty bucks. The reading took place on September 11, 2001, and I shared the stage that night with a woman who did a whole cycle of poems devoted to her "perfect pussy" while cars formed a line that circled the block around the gas station across the street, because, you know, it was 9/11. My poems were mainly fake Buddhism and poorly disguised sex fantasies. Neither of us, for a moment, acted like what we were doing wasn't the most important thing.

I took a year off after my undergrad (and by that I mean did not get accepted into either the teaching program or the MFA writing program I applied to) and wrote and read poetry for hours every day. I wasn't just a writer, I was a poet—or fast becoming one.

Then my dad died, and I couldn't find the muscle that wrote poems. That was like fifteen years ago and I've written two poems since, both about birds. I started writing prose, essays, and stuff that no one read, and stuff that wasn't for reading, other stuff I sent bouncing out and around the world. Without an audience, without a discipline, I kept writing, found the voice of my writing. That badge on my chest that said "writer" sunk into me, became permanent. I will never not write. I know this.

I remember, when Becca was still pregnant with Ollie, thinking about how one day this kid would make an original work of art. We would have made a thing that would make a thing. My first year of college was probably the first time I wrote something truly creative. I cared so much about my writing before that, but it was really not much more than tracing.

Art is the closest I get to believing in anything like magic. I was raised in an unreligious house. The handful of times I went to any church growing up involved weddings, funerals, and that one friend who had a house rule that if someone slept over on Saturday they had to go to church on Sunday before going home (looking back on it, this is a pretty creepy rule).

So I grew up indifferent to religion as a set of beliefs or even as ritual. Becca grew up Catholic, and though she's no longer in the church, she fills in that space with small practices that mean something to her. She'll light a candle when a loved person is going through a hard time, she'll do Tarot or horoscopes sometimes, and when we talk about them she lets on like she believes a little less than she does and I act like I believe a little more than I do. Really, I believe in none of it, in nothing, except maybe in art.

I don't like being an atheist. I would love to be able to believe that there's a god and, more than that, that there's an afterlife. I'd give anything to believe that, even if it wasn't true. I guess I'd love for there to be a plan, a meaning. I don't. I hate it, but I can't stop not believing.

I had a dream once that I was back in school, a student at the high school where I used to teach but in an art class taught by my high school art teacher, Mr. Barder. He was showing us pottery, these intricate bowls, and asking if any of us believed that the bowls were alive. A lot of the class did. I didn't. He asked about it, and I stood and went on this long speech to him about wishing I could . . . that being alive meant having thoughts, movement, direction, and if you didn't believe, there was no kind of alive, no piece of aliveness. You are alive or you are not at all. I started to tell him this was the basis of my fear of death, but I stopped, unwilling to broach the subject even in dreams. I asked for help to see and believe more than I do. He told me he'd help, every so often showing me a piece of art that was particularly *beautiful,* particularly *alive.* He used those words as synonyms. There was an idea, in the dream, that engaging with that art over time and purposefully would perhaps help me to see beyond some binary of alive/not alive.

I guess that's why art is so important to me. If the world is just matter clumped together by chance and gravity, if people are just accidents of evolution, and if love and fear and hope are just chemical reactions, then none of this really matters. But then, what is art? What is art doing in all that mess? It is more powerful, more useful, more beautiful than it has any right to be, and it gives us a lens to see all those other pieces as more powerful and useful and beautiful than they have any right to be. In that way, to me it is magic, an outlet, at least, for some form of belief.

If you doubt the magic of it, watch your kid make art sometime, watch any young person make art sometime.

When I started teaching, I was desperate to work in an arts school. From my own experience going through schools, I guessed that typical schools had maybe one serious artist every three years, and that was not enough. At the time, my state only had two arts schools, and I somehow landed a job at one of them. Working there meant that a good portion of my students identified as artists of some kind, and they all had two hours a day where they could practice some of those arts. The school, though it offered classes in visual art, media art, theater, dance, choir, band, and orchestra, offered no creative writing classes. Fine with me. I would infuse it into my Language Arts class, as well as using my Arts-World experience to mix in multidisciplinary projects.

Some of the art I saw from middle schoolers during those years was incredible. There was a comic strip essay one student made that is framed and in my room that included illustrations that looked professional, a bit like the ink line drawings of old Batman comics, with the hero, Mr. English Teacher Man, fighting nameless foes while discussing with them the visual metaphors of the graphic novel *MAUS*. There were two solo dances, done in different years at the end-of-the-year performance that both brought me to tears with their ability to communicate so much of what each artist had to say that wouldn't fit into words. There were video projects that still get talked about among teachers who worked there, one by a group of students who called themselves The Gallon because they were four leaders. (Get it? Four liters in a gallon.) There's the ink-and-wash drawing one student did that felt so perfect to me I got it as a tattoo on my right forearm. There was art, so much art, that was created by these young people and could have existed in spaces alongside professional art done by adults. There was a marker of quality to things that, honestly, rightly, made me embarrassed of my rhyming poems from high school.

When I moved to the arts high school, there were still students who performed or created at those heightened levels, students who would no doubt pursue careers or a lifetime focus on the arts, but there were a lot more kids to which art was more a hobby than a passion, and plenty more who were just there for small class sizes. I went through a period of concern for the program, that it wasn't living up to its potential as a *real* arts school, that we surely could do something to instill in more of our students the sort of fervor I carried for the arts, that we could attract more *real* artists.

It didn't take me too long to realize that I was being an ass. We had always had conversations among the staff about product versus process, with different teachers landing on far ends of that spectrum, a dance teacher who would deliver polished performances that students drilled and drilled on under high pressure worked right alongside a theater teacher who would occasionally have students perform bizarre and experimental works of unfinished stuff that students had written and directed and torn apart and thrown together.

I started out firmly on Team Product, interested in the quality that could be produced by young people when given time and resources and access to talented adults (who kinda actually did some of the hardest stuff for them). I am now the captain of Team Process. In my years in the high school, and reflecting on the years before, I started to see a gap between the impression of best art that was shown off outside of our school and the importance of all the messy art we kept hidden in the rooms.

The real power of arts in schools didn't really hit me until I started work in my current school, because we don't do very much of it at all. There's a visual arts program (with, really, some of the very best art teachers I've ever worked with), and there's band and choir, but not everyone does those, and not every year. More than that, my old district had art infusion as one of their main instructional goals, to the point that there was a fully stocked empty art room that classroom teachers could check out for projects and stuff. (One year, a sixth grade class built a canoe in there.) In my new building, artistic projects in academic classes are pretty rare, and so when students are asked to draw or act or make stuff, I'm often met with a whole lot of "I don't know how" or "I'm not any good."

In a school that did a lot more art a lot more often, I saw students who were a lot more comfortable with failure, a lot more comfortable with risk and with vulnerability. Sometimes, our great dancers were awful at drawing but would do so if asked. We had plenty of introverted, quiet visual artists who would have preferred to keep drawing eyes in their notebooks forever than have to take part in a dance or a puppet show, or, terror of all terrors, write some spoken word, but they would do it. Working outside of our specialties is important. Sucking at drawing and doing it anyway teaches you a lot, even if your drawings never get better.

Without a lot of chances to practice something you aren't great at, it can be really scary every time you're asked to do so. Art helps that. Without access to space and time and projects that give you a chance to express yourself, investigate the world, or find a voice, all those things can be too scary to try when you need them most. Art helps that. With fewer opportunities to know their classmates for more things, not just athletics and academics, but creativity and humor and perspective, it's harder to see and celebrate the value in each kid. Art helps with that.

I'm just as big a proponent of art in education as I've ever been, just as sure of its power to shape and save and enhance lives (whether it is me, writing well before I had anything worth reading, or Ollie, sending art to places across the world almost a decade before they're allowed to drive there). I'm less and less worried about whether the art we do in schools is any good, and more and more sure that it's good for us.

As a generally literate though not very academic white guy, I am contractually obligated to believe that Kurt Vonnegut is much greater than he probably is. He said once in a speech (saying it was a teacher who told him, though I imagine he used *teacher* and *uncle* the way I'm using *aunt*) that the job of an artist is to make one piece of the universe "exactly as it should be."

The part of me that reacts poorly to a lack of control is comforted, then, by an empty page I get that kind of power over.

I often think of my writing as a reaction to something wrong with me. I picture it as a complex clockwork-type mechanism somewhere between my heart and stomach whose only job is to wind a piece of string tighter and tighter around a spool. Each day I don't write, the machine works a little harder, for a little longer, until the string and the little wooden gears and everything are about to snap and fall completely apart. Then I write something, even something small, but I make a little block of words do exactly what I want them to do, and the thing unwinds and I can breathe normally for a short time while it starts to slowly respool that string. In that way it is art that keeps me healthy, whether anyone is reading it or not. The quality of the thing is important to the writer part of me, but the control of something, no matter how small, is what unwinds the string before I snap.

Hi, my name is Tom. I like writing metaphors for my anxiety.

DECEMBER

ANXIETY TIME

I DON'T DO SO GREAT IN THE WINTER.
When the days get shorter and darker, and when being outside hurts, and when social events with too many people trying too hard to be too happy pile one on top of the other during holidays, I don't do great. December is the start of my high-anxiety time and has been since before I even knew what that was.

My first anxiety attack was during French class in my second year of college. I was not good at speaking French, which is quite likely due to me being exceptionally awful at listening or trying in French. My mind was wandering in class, and I've since forgotten how it started, but it must have jumped from French to music to that girl I talked to in that one class to maybe poems to I'm hungry to holy shit I'm going to die really for real die someday shit shit shit. The class ended and I sat there as the room emptied, too frightened to move, barely able to breathe, just sat and oh shit shit shit shit shit in my head until I somehow stood, stumbled home, walked back to my apartment with the world looking like a movie I was watching through a hole in a wall.

Over the next few days, things did not get very much better. My stomach felt like it had been completely removed. I didn't eat, struggled to sleep. Absolutely nothing I did or thought about or ate or created felt like it carried even a small sliver of meaning next to this one ultimate truth. Every person in my life felt a mile away. I didn't understand why we weren't all just screaming in fear of death every moment.

What snapped me out of it, and I'm not sure how or why it did, was that that Saturday I went with Becca and my roommates to a weekly midnight cabaret. Performers sign up at the door, and nothing is ever screened or censored. (The cabaret is called BALLS Cabaret, after Leslie Ball, its founder, and is the place in Minneapolis where I have seen some of the most beautiful and powerful art and people, and where I spent many years going and reading new poems and goofy stories and stuff like that. For a few years there, I almost never missed a show.) At the end of this particular night, which I had spent staring blankly at the stage, still trapped deep in my own little fear jail, there was a dance performance. I am no great dance critic, but something about this dance, which was a lot of scarves and jumping and rolling and scarves, tickled many of us a great deal. It was bad. Bad bad. So awful it was beautiful, so big in its absurdity, a sort of drunken orgasm while attempting to dodge an invisible laser security system and also have scarves sort of vibe, that I forgot to think of anything else other than "What the fuck."

When the dance ended, my little group clapped respectfully and made our way from the theater where we walked purposefully and silently around a corner before we stopped to laugh. I am not usually one to laugh at anyone's attempt at art, I swear, and neither was anyone else there, I swear. But we laughed. I doubled over against the wall, laughing hard enough my stomach hurt, but also enough that my stomach unclenched enough for the first time in a week that I felt present and alive and something other than terrified. We laughed for a few long minutes, then gathered ourselves together, noticing only then that our group included a person who we didn't even know, a slightly older woman who was in the audience and had followed us around the corner. She patted my shoulder and as she walked away, still breathing hard from the laughing, she said, "Oh, I needed that."

Me too, it turned out. Me too. I wasn't all better by any means, but I had at least reopened a door to some normalcy in my body and brain, had introduced the idea that I wouldn't need to feel permanently and always awful.

I have always struggled with anxiety in some way, but for the next couple of months I was nearly consumed by it. Any small moment where I felt a loss of control, including any caffeine, a bus that was three minutes late, a sweater getting stuck over my head as I took it off, demolished me. My heart would race, I would struggle to breathe anything but shallow breaths, I'd get so wrapped up in my thoughts I would need to jump around and wave my arms to remind myself I was in a body.

There were a couple of times when some of my darkest thoughts snuck in. I wished I hadn't been born so that I could have avoided the fear of death. I was not suicidal, but was whatever the opposite of that is, so scared of death that I did almost nothing that looked like living. I had some of the oddest thoughts, like considering doing more than just writing to leave evidence of my life and impact on the world, like perhaps starting to keep jars of urine in my room as a way to hold on to every part of my precious and fragile life just a little bit longer. I mean, I didn't do it. I didn't. But I had the impulse.

I've never told anyone that. But now I wrote it. Okay.

I've put in a lot of work since then toward managing my anxiety so that it is more like my asshole uncle on Facebook. I can usually let it flare up, sigh, and move on, but every so often it sneaks under my skin and ruins a whole damn day or two. I know all the little tricky ways it shows up, too; sometimes as an overreaction to something moderately annoying, and sometimes, completely unrelated to anything, feeling like something (or everything) is about to go horribly wrong.

It's also the superpower that keeps me from getting too relaxed with my work or my writing, that makes me keep writing and working harder and more. In the final stages of my previous book I stopped taking my medication because I wanted to work on it as raw as possible, because there's an energy to that that I feel is important to the biggest things I have to say. It was a bad idea. I'll probably do it again for this book, and it will be a bad idea then, too.

I've seen these things in Ollie. In the crying that can't stop, yes, which was dismissed for years as small kid/big feelings stuff. The night it really sunk in was a lot less dramatic than a full-blown anxiety attack.

Ollie doesn't sleep well. They never have. As a very young one, this meant constant trips from our bed to theirs, and bedtime routines that were and continue to be long and ridiculous. At a younger age, they would be crying or yelling for us, and we would come in to requests for water, for more blankets, for less blankets, for a snack, to help find the stuffed bunny that was lying just to the side of Ollie's shoulder. As they've gotten older, the requests are not much different, but now Ollie will wander the house to find us. There are headaches or hurting stomachs, or the kinds of questions that pop in a kid's head when they are quiet enough to let them.

There are also nights, like that one night, when the things keeping Ollie awake sound all too familiar to me. Walking from their room to find me at the kitchen table, they said, "I'm so tired." This is of course the exact sort of thing that is a problem *at bedtime* and worthy of a trip out of bed to alert me. Usually, we would laugh at that sort of thing, because Ollie is game for being called out on being ridiculous, but their face was too serious, so I asked what was really up.

"I want to go to sleep, but it's like I'm really scared, and there's no reason to be, but I'm scared anyway."

Oh. Yeah. I know that one.

So Ollie has anxiety, has that piece of their brain that works a lot like mine does. That is sometimes an uncomfortable feeling that something is going wrong unattached to our actual circumstances, and sometimes much much worse than that.

I fucking hate when Ollie has anxiety attacks. The first one we named as such was when the music teacher sent Ollie to the nurse so they could try to breathe normally again, but they've happened a number of times since. Ollie feels too cold and then too hot. They feel like something awful is about to happen or, I suppose more specifically, that something awful is actively happening, even though nothing is. Sometimes they are brought on by nothing, by a moment, a pause, a stillness in the day (but usually the night) by something that catches just wrong. Sometimes it's just a thing that got out of control, out of their control. It's a schedule change that wasn't announced, or a big event (even a big happy event) that is impending, and the biggness of it is too much, and then Ollie is having trouble breathing normally, suddenly sucks in on themselves. There is stomach pain, and everything is too big, too loud, too much, like every part of them is a wound. It's awful. I fucking hate it.

I hate it because I hate to see Ollie in pain, and in pain in a way that I cannot apply a bandage, cannot find the source of the pain and punch it. It just sucks, and I can't make it stop. It sucks most because . . . fuck.

Because I look at Ollie, I watch Ollie miserable and folded and shaking, and I feel, I *know,* that I did this. I gave this to them. My. Fucking. Fault.

I know all the reasons not to say that, not to feel that. I tell myself these things, tell myself that I am doing everything I can to help Ollie to handle their anxiety, tell myself it may not have come from me, tell myself flimsy lies about how their anxiety may well just go away someday. These things do not help. When I see Ollie's anxiety, I see my anxiety, a perfect mirror image of my anxiety. I know that I have passed it on to them.

And hey, wanna know what's fun? Guess what that does for my anxiety? Nothing brings a family together like a pair of panic attacks, right?

But I'm also best at helping Ollie when they're going through it, because I know exactly how it feels, and I have, like, twenty years under my belt getting my ass kicked by my brain. I know a little bit what helps and what doesn't. I usually catch it half a second before Becca does, and of course I am there for Ollie for every bit of it, and then Becca helps with the aftermath and the aftercare, and I find a quiet corner of the house somewhere to feel like my lungs are squeezing hard around my heart.

It was a long time, years after the maybe-pee-into-jars step on my anxiety path, that I even named my anxiety. Later still that I could identify it in the times it was harming but not incapacitating me.

As a young teacher, I would have moments in class where I could feel my heart, could look down and see my heartbeat visibly shaking the picture on my ID badge that made me look like a ska band bass player. I could say that I was half-sure I was going to die, but that's more average than accurate. One part of my brain was 100 percent sure I was going to die, the other was, like, "You always think that, Tom, and you haven't died yet." I kept teaching because as a young teacher I felt like if I wasn't ever teaching or thinking about teaching for even one minute, then everything would crumble around me and I would fail forever.

Did I mention that anxiety is fun? So, really, those moments were about two kinds of anxiety. The first is the sort of all-the-time fun where my brain does what my friend Shanna calls "awfulizing." That's the anxiety muscle that keeps me sure that everyone hates what I just said in a meeting. The other anxiety is the emergency alert system, the I-and-everyone-else-is-about-to-die system, only squirrels keep setting it off at night, and there are lights and horns and scared sentries firing into the darkness.

When I was teaching, the alarms would go off and I did my best to power through them. I'd be a less good teacher all day because it's very hard to show grace and patience when your body is screaming I'M DYING at you all day. I'd go home, my whole body a fist, and slowly wind down until I was relaxed enough, just before bed usually, to start shivering and shaking. Becca would put an arm around me when I let her, and I would say something like, "I think this has been happening all day." Of course it had. I just didn't know what to call it. I knew what anxiety attacks were, but only in that I knew that other people had them.

The tricky thing about anxiety is that it can be really hard to see in yourself, because the probably heart attack you're imagining feels like a very real probable heart attack. So it can be a lot easier to see in others, which is how I made my first anxiety buddy.

Lexi didn't get to have an anxiety condition, because she's Black.

I mean, of course she had an anxiety condition, but there's a callousness I've seen toward the mental health of kids of color in many schools I've been in. When the white girl's hamster dies, friends are allowed out of class to hug her in a big group in the hallway. When the black girl loses a parent to cancer, teachers talk three days later about how it's about time for her to start getting things back to normal.

There was a day that I was walking out of my classroom, and Lexi was sitting on the ground, her back against her locker, her head between her knees. I could see her hands shaking.

"Hey," I said, because I'm not smart, "are you okay?"

"I'm not breathing," she said, her voice shaking worse than her hands.

That got me to stop, drop to a knee, and look around for any actually responsible adult I could pull in to help me. There was none.

"You can't breathe?"

"I can. I just can't."

"Do you have asthma?"

"No, but this—" There was a pause for a short spasm of a breath between almost every word. Scared, quick tears were racing each other down her face. "Happens. Sometimes. I can't make myself breathe right."

I didn't know what to do, but I know what I'd seen on TV. So I got her a brown paper bag from my room, and she breathed into it. I think it's supposed to show that your breath is working? I don't know. She tried, breathing in and out of it three or four times before she dropped the bag on the floor, sunk her head back between her knees, her shoulders shaking now.

"Didn't work?"

She looked up at me, the shoulder shaking now obviously from laughing, and said, "That's the dumbest thing I've ever done." Then we both laughed. I sat on the floor next to her, and we talked about anything other than what had just happened, just chatted. Her voice calmed way before her hands. It was five minutes, maybe ten, until she looked mostly normal. She eventually stood, ready to make her way back to whatever class she had run out of when the whole thing had started. I promised to walk her there, act as her pass, and make sure she wasn't in trouble.

She apologized for her "freak-out."

I told her not to worry about that, really, I had things like that happen to me kinda often, too.

"Really? Where you can't breathe and you feel like you're going to die for no reason?"

"Exactly like that. I think it's an anxiety attack." Saying the words to Lexi was the first time I admitted it to myself. Those things I was having? Those were anxiety attacks.

"They suck," she said.

"They do. Yes. You feeling better now?"

"I mean, it's not better, but it's better, you know?"

I knew.

Lexi and I became anxiety buddies. I was the adult she had at school who understood and could help as much as could be helped. Sometimes I'd just tell her, "Man, had a tough one yesterday," and she'd say, "Sucks," and that would be it. She'd do the same; I'd ask if she needed anything that day, and she'd usually say no. As I got more and more comfortable naming and discussing my anxiety, that year and after, I became more open with it in my classroom. I've had quite a few anxiety buddies since I started talking about it to my classes at the beginning of the year. With no actual training or anything, I try hard not to be the only place a kid can go and direct them toward some help if they need it, but I'm very happy to be one additional place they go when a day is a bad day.

Very recently, Olive came and found me in the house and stood near me and made a sound, a sort of "hmmph" that translates to "Something is wrong and please fix it for me." I asked Ollie what was up, and they said, "You know that feeling where there's a loud noise, and it's there for long enough that you get used to it, and then when the sound stops, the silence feels really weird and bad?

I've been feeling like that for the past two days. Do you think it's anxiety?"

Yes, I waited, like, three thousand words into this chapter before giving you that, the most perfect description of anxiety ever. In the moment it was hard not to reward them for the poetic specificity of their statement, such is my word nerdery, but I didn't. I said that, yeah, that sounded a heck of a lot like anxiety to me, and then I asked all the questions I get pissed at when someone asks me, like "Did something bad happen?" and "Are you worried about anything in particular?" But nothing was happening and nothing was scary or more worrying than normal, and instead their body just felt bad, like something bad was happening or about to happen.

So we both smoked a joint and felt a lot better.

Kidding. Nothing in the world triggers my anxiety like smok—. You know what, never mind.

Point being, even though I'd been living with it for decades, there wasn't much I knew to do to really help Olive. I had some ideas of things that had helped me, and Becca, being a therapist, had some very good ideas and things to practice that may help, but also we are Olive's parents and therefore know nothing about anything most of the time. Luckily, Olive had some good experiences with a therapist once before and asked if they could go again, this time to specifically talk about anxiety. Double luckily, we were at a place where we could afford for that to happen.

And so Ollie, only fifteen or so years earlier than I did, had named their anxiety, had understood it was something they could work to make better, had asked for help to do that. It's a truly remarkable thing, and one that young people seem to be getting better and better at the more we do to destigmatize mental illness.

We may well be living in the age of anxiety. Everything from big national studies to conversations with my school counselor are telling me that it is showing up more and more in our kids. At first

I thought we were getting better at naming it, maybe, which may well be a piece of it; but also, it just seems to be surfacing more, more severely, than before.

In my classroom, there's no pattern I can find of who is impacted most, no kind of kid who predictably shows more anxiety. There's just more. Schools are getting better at helping kids, to be sure, but not nearly all schools and not nearly well enough. Schools are a bad place to be anxious, a bad place to have a brain telling you to do or feel anything different from those around you. It's a system, and the people are the parts. The system works best when the people all do what they're supposed to, and far too often our reflex is to shame or punish any person slowing the system down.

I have a student in my class who, though bright and curious about the world, was not super engaged in my class. On some days, sure, he was with us and doing group work and all that. He usually got stuff done on time, too, but there were days where he just seemed to sit and stare.

So as someone who has anxiety, who understands what it looks like and all the different ways that it can present itself, I did exactly the wrong thing and just yelled at the kid a bunch to get to work, to try harder, to do more. I was reading his detachment as disrespect, had pegged him as the kind of kid who just floats through school and needs a kick in the ass every so often. (It should be said that I have never taught one student who just needed to get yelled at every so often in order to find their passion for learning. That doesn't mean I don't keep trying, though, because I am very good at this teaching thing.)

Being a jackass to this kid didn't seem to help at all, and then one day I was on the way across the room and noticed him sitting and staring at a blank screen. I literally, actually, and for real opened my mouth to do some more super-effective jackassery and caught this little squint of his eye, almost too quick to see, but the kind that looked like a reaction to some sharp pain. He hadn't seen me yet, wasn't talking to anyone at his table, but was just, for some reason, hurting.

I kept walking over to him, but instead of "Get to work," I asked, "Is everything okay?" I asked it like I meant it, because I did. I sometimes catch myself forgetting that I actually care a lot about each and every kid in my room when I get tired or frustrated or wrapped up in some project or some marker of completion. It makes me more tired, more frustrated, and it certainly isn't helping the kids in the room. When moments like these happen, moments where I catch myself, reorient myself, moments when I remind myself to lead with the care I feel, it helps. It helps to remind myself how important so many moments, so many interactions can be with students, and how badly I want to waste as few of them as I can.

He told me he was having a rough day but was fine, was having trouble focusing. I told him it was okay to have a rough day, that the work could wait if he needed some time. I asked if I could do anything, could help at all, but he said no.

It wasn't a big thing, a ten-second conversation that communicated care instead of completion. It didn't make whatever thing all better. There weren't hallway conversations with tears and hugs. He seemed to feel a little better, and so did I. You can't make it better, but you can make it better, you know?

WHAT DO WE DO WITH SMART KIDS?

WHEN I SWITCHED TO MY NEW SCHOOL, I was asked if I would be willing to take a sixth grader into my eighth grade Language Arts class. Normally, I stay away from sixth graders at all costs. It is the last of the years that kids will line up cat figurines on their desk and openly pick their nose and wipe their boogers on their shirts. So I wasn't overly enthused about the prospect of not just having one of the little ones around, but somehow mixing him with a bunch of eighth graders.

Before this all happened with my own kid, I think I felt the way about the "gifted" kids that a lot of people do, which is the way that a lot of our schools treat them. I thought, "Meh. Those kids are fine."

But they aren't, not always.

The thinking from the school was this: sixth grade has two separate classes, Reading and Language Arts. Language Arts focuses a lot on writing and grammar, and Reading focuses on, you know, reading. This sixth grader coming in was testing way higher than middle school as a reader and felt confident in his ability to keep up with the work. He was also obviously looking for a challenge. He had started teaching himself Swahili the year before and succeeded to the level that his parents got him a tutor to continue his studies. The seventh grade teacher was brand-new to teaching, and admin felt more comfortable having him in my class for the year. So, yeah, let's go for it.

Right in the middle of all this work with Ollie, working to understand why a normal school program probably wasn't going to work for them and what it meant to have the kind of brain they have, I also had Steven, every day in my room, doing way more than just keeping up with his older classmates. It was hard not to compare Ollie and Steven, and to worry that I wasn't doing for Steven what Ollie would have needed if they were in my class.

When our year ended, Steven would be headed down the hall to high school classes for Language Arts (we share a building, so it's pretty easy). Also, my god, this gets so complex and shitty. Basically, a year before the ninth grade teachers were told they couldn't have honors or regular English 9 anymore, that, instead, they should offer a class that gives each student access to honors-level work so that more will consider honors and AP classes later in high school. The teachers hated the move. They wanted honors back.

The move to make honors-level work available to all students lasted the totality of one year. When the district told them, "Making an honors track in ninth grade that leads to AP classes later means that fewer kids take AP later. Let's have all students do pre-AP work," they heard, "All of your students will now be able to do honors in the exact same way as you've always taught it, so teach it to all of them." The result, I was told, was not honors for all but, rather, honors for none.

The ninth grade team complained that students weren't able to do honors-level Language Arts. It seemed to me it had more to do with students not being able to do honors the way they were being asked. In a meeting I was told that my class and style were not rigorous enough to prepare students. That same day a ninth grader was in my room after school working on their homework, which was a word-find about the parts of a story. We, my colleagues and I, have very different definitions of what *rigorous* means. We also have very different definitions of what *honors* students should be like.

Eventually, I was told, they started "adapting" the class by slowing things down and shortening assignments, by making things more simple. The district relented and gave them back their honors class, and it was up to us to figure out who would get in and who wouldn't. With the start of the new calendar year, choices had to be made soon before kids started registering. This was after a few meetings where I raised my voice more than I was proud of, but also where it was eventually confirmed that we were working from two very different and contrary philosophies. Ultimately, no matter what small changes we make, I'll be helping to institute a practice that I think is wrong and unfair. I really really hate that.

Because, yeah, I think tracking is in most cases damaging to nearly every kid involved. I've taught classes in middle and high school and have always taught untracked classes. The district I came up in didn't believe in an honors track, and I got to see the power of keeping kids together. It maybe takes a little more work as a teacher, or at least a shifting of perspective as a teacher, to allow for a wide range of abilities in the room. I should be fair and say that it seems like it would be a lot harder in Math, and also I don't understand how to teach math at all.

In Language Arts classes, I'm pretty used to having kids in a single room who have a ten-year gap in their reading level. (Say what you want about reading levels and grade levels and all that: the tests can't be so screwed up that when it says one kid reads at a second-grade level and one at a twelfth, they actually have similar skill sets.) My goal always is to give them access to honors-level work, honors-level thinking, and not because every single kid is ready to read four chapters a night and do the worksheet before class the next day, but because kids are smart in all sorts of different ways, and often that second-grade-level reader knows a bunch of stuff or sees a bunch of stuff that the other kids don't, which means that to have them together you may have to adapt what they read or write or how fast or whatever. So if every kid needs a slightly different honors class in order to have them all together, that's what we should give them.

Sometimes this means I do a lot of choice or varied reading. For example, everyone will be reading to practice critical analysis. We'll spend time deconstructing and analyzing music videos first as a way to introduce the concept. We'll watch Beyonce's "Formation" and Bomba Estereo's "Soy Yo" and a few others. Deconstruction is a process a lot of students aren't super good at because, at least from what I've seen, their brains jump to find meaning or at least a judgment about something. So practicing deconstruction, making students pause and write down details without analysis of a video, is good for everyone.

Because the activity involves not a lot of reading but a mode of thinking new to most of them, students start on equal ground. This is fun because sometimes, actually pretty often, those students used to getting things quickly and cashing in work for quick As in lots of classes struggle with looking at texts and art as abstractions to be studied. It can be a tough year for those kids, because eighth grade is also when they are being introduced to more abstract math ideas. For kids used to thinking super concretely and being rewarded for coming up with (or remembering) the right answer the quickest, it can be a struggle to be told to slow down, think harder, dig deeper, and engage in conversations where there are not always clear answers.

In lots of years, I've seen those concrete "good-kid" students struggle with the abstract stuff and then learn and be led by those students they are used to outperforming. In the same class as Steven,

I had one of those kids that teachers talk about as being "absolutely the best, unless you're trying to teach him something." Harrison is a super polite, thoughtful kid, the kind who would remember that you said last Wednesday that your mom was going in for knee surgery during the weekend and then would ask you on Monday how she was doing. He was half a foot shorter than most of his classmates, but his hair shot up from his head almost high enough to compensate. He was used to lots of attention and not great grades, and, I gathered, he was used to every single day of school being a whole lot of fun except for parent/teacher conferences.

We did okay at the beginning of the year together, and as a generally goofy pain in the ass myself, I read his easy grasp of humor and people and his energy and enthusiasm for everything (except things that involved sitting still) as all the things that made school hard for him and all the things that were likely to make him successful in the future. I told his mom exactly that at fall conferences and she almost cried. She was not used to hearing anyone other than herself say that her son was smart and talented and good. But he was. He proved it, ten times over, when we hit the critical analysis part of the year.

Harrison absolutely killed it at analysis, many times dragging his classmates along past low-level observations ("They use lots of bright colors") to some truly staggeringly hot takes ("This is commentary on how Black people are all different from each other, but also a strong community"). When we moved to reading high-level texts (in this case, MLK's "Letter from Birmingham Jail"), Harrison kept it up, comparing King's critique of white moderates to his own community's reaction to Philando Castille's killing.

The Birmingham Jail lesson is used as a way to scaffold the class from analyzing videos to text. Students read the text in small groups on a shared Google doc multiple times through, first identifying words or phrases they don't understand, then building understanding of those things, then looking for things like themes, important quotes, and main ideas. Students who are reading at a higher level often do some heavier lifting on decoding the text the first round through, but most students can engage evenly on text-based analysis after that.

When we get to our final assessment for the unit, students choose a novel (with some coaching) to write a critical analysis essay on. I work with every kid on the book they are choosing, push them to pick something that will work for the assignment and is appropriately challenging for them. One student who struggled more with reading read Neil Gaiman's *Marvel 1602* comic. Other students read *The Hate U Give* and *Aristotle and Dante Discover the Secrets of the Universe* and other high-quality young-adult novels. Students who were ready to push on read novels like *Kindred* and *The Things They Carried*.

Steven read *A Brief History of the Universe* the first time through the project. He also read *Children of Blood and Bone* and *Their Eyes Were Watching God* over the course of the year. His essays were always spectacular, and though he was pretty quiet in class conversations, it was obvious he was not struggling with the shift to abstract thinking. In fact, he seemed pretty excited to have the challenge. I'm not sure that I always gave him enough that stretched him like that. It's not that he always looked bored, but he certainly didn't always look, I dunno, *activated*. He was polite about it, about everything, and his parents were always supportive of our class, but, ugh—it didn't always feel like enough.

I do know that it was great to have Steven and Harrison together. Harrison, the eighth grade super popular Black boy, and Steven, the quiet redheaded sixth grader, have brains that work very differently from one another, have brains that show up very differently on tests, show up very differently in classroom spaces, and are also both super fucking brilliant in the ways that they are brilliant.

They'll both be in ninth grade Language Arts next year, but Steven will be heading to the newly reinstated honors class. Harrison didn't even try to take the test to get in. I hate that. Those two brains should be together, and kids with brains like Steven, with brains like Olive, should grow up learning that kids who don't read as fast as they do, or do math as well, or get good grades or good test scores, are not necessarily less smart and certainly have input and perspective and ideas and answers that should be listened to and taken seriously. Neither Ollie nor Steven have shown any sign of that kind of intellectual snobbery, but I'm worried. Ollie is still young enough to grow up to be a jerk.

To be clear, Ollie is not a jerk now, not even close. Even in those early years when kids are naturally huge dickheads, Ollie was constantly (or at least very nearly constantly) aware of the feelings of those around them and has really never said a disparaging word about anyone at school. I like to think this has to do with the parenting work we've done, like when Ollie came home talking about students in their class who were disruptive to the point of being destructive, and we were able to explain to Ollie that the student likely was missing all the help they needed and so needed some compassion from their classmates. But also Ollie is just Ollie, so that when we explained those things, Ollie responded, "Oh well, I try to sit by him during lunch and ask him to play at recess, but I'm also not going to stop telling him that it's wrong to bully other kids."

Which is, yeah, the correct answer. But I'm also aware that while Ollie is very consciously empathetic and interested in lots of people, they may be getting messages on a subconscious level about who is smart and who isn't and what that means. I worry about those same things with tracking (or detracking without doing the work to really give each kid the support and space to succeed).

In their old school, Ollie was bored out of their mind throughout every day. Part of that was pacing, sure, content that Ollie grasped quickly that other kids needed more time with. A lot of it was the worksheets and worksheets and worksheets, was the lack of choice and space to explore and build and ask questions.

So I'm against tracking, but I am more against boredom. Also, students need classes where they get to be around kids like them and kids not like them, and also should be intellectually challenged and emotionally supported. The easy answer is separating kids out; the best answer for Olive is the program they are now in, but we could do a whole heck of a lot better than that for everyone.

In the past few months of the new school, Ollie's class has been working on science fair projects. Ollie's original idea involved having two sets of friends play different games at recess, one playing human games and the other playing games dogs play. They were trying to show why dogs are happier than people, but it was shot down for involving human test subjects. (An argument can be made that elementary kids should not be encouraged to do science experiences on each other, but, you know, if you're going to make an omelet . . .) Ollie's current project is to develop a backpack for cats who roam. This backpack could (but will not) contain a GPS to help find the cat. Instead, the owner will be able to press a button and have food drop out of the backpack so they don't have to worry about the cat needing food while it adventures.

Students have also made Rube Goldberg machines, written a class play with a professional storyteller, read a bunch of books of their own choosing, and had class discussions about a few they all read. They learned under the direction of teachers who expected them to work hard and be challenged, encouraged them to struggle and fail, and who understood each one of them as complex humans. None of these things should be restricted to "gifted" education.

The class has a lot in common with tons of elementary schools all over the country, sure, but if stuff like that had been happening a lot more at Ollie's old school, had they found better ways to challenge Ollie academically while giving time to questioning or building or problem solving or leadership skills that other kids have who don't always read super fast or teach themselves to code, we may never have left.

My very first year of teaching, I had this kid Sam. As teachers, we remember kids for all kinds of different reasons, but the kids we remember fondly do often tend to be kids who do well in our classes. Not Sam. Sam failed four straight quarters of eighth-grade English under my direction. She was never even close to passing.

This had a lot to do with how I was grading at the time. You see, Sam is probably one of the smartest kids I've ever taught and certainly the smartest kid I've ever failed. Sam read Shakespeare like it was a children's book, wrote beautifully and passionately when she wanted to, and more than any of that, saw how language worked like she was Neo, seeing the Matrix as code. What Sam didn't do was any damn thing she didn't feel like doing, and she never felt like turning in homework. So though she consistently showed me in class that she was understanding everything we did, the gradebook showed only a row of zeros.

I've since adjusted my grading, and I'm pretty sure Sam's grade would now represent what she actually knew and could do, not just her ability to complete things and turn them in. But, you know, grades matter less than what you actually learn, especially in middle school. I worry that Sam learned early on that we couldn't or wouldn't teach her all that much, that instead we'd do a lot of stressing about points.

We didn't and we don't do a lot of talking about what kids like Sam or Ollie or Steven need. But watching Ollie's energy and excitement for school return once they went to a school that understands them, that challenges them to think, really think about what they are learning and why and how, has me thinking more and more about the sort of schools all kids deserve.

With Sam, nearly every adult would go through a process of first treating her like she was somehow unable to do the work she didn't do, slowing things down or shortening them, then by showing kindness and concern about home or about friends, talking about deadline extensions and recovering points, and then slowly, sometimes very slowly, would realize they had a kid who may damn well be a genius in their class. This process no doubt took longer because Sam is Black. Teachers saw Olive's skills more readily than struggles no doubt because Olive is white.

We saw a specialist early on in the process of finding Ollie the right place. She warned us that kids with their kind of intellectual intensity don't just "get by" in programs that aren't right for them. There's a lot of gifted kids who aren't "fine" in a typical classroom. Without real learning, without real outlets for their intellect and understanding about their sensitivities, those kinds of kids are very likely to burn out, to shut down, to self-destruct. I can't help but feel guilty about all the kids who are like Ollie but without all the privileges Ollie had to be recognized, to have support and access, to be believed when they showed signs of needing something different. I can't help but feel guilty about all the Olives we miss.

FEBRUARY

SO WHITE

OUR EXTENDED WORK ON "LETTER FROM Birmingham Jail" usually keeps my inbox pretty empty. Talking about Martin Luther King Jr. is one of those things, like Shakespeare, that's pretty unassailable by even the most upset-est parent. What usually gets the emails rolling in this time of year is that while talking about MLK, we also talk about race and racism. I mean . . . how dare we, right?

Yes, I get emails about how MLK wouldn't want us to talk about race. Ugh. Professionalism dictates that I don't get to answer those emails saying what I would like to, which is, "Please find yourself a Google and use it." No, I need to be a big kid and explain that talking about and studying racism doesn't conjure it into existence, and, in fact, ignoring it can be very damaging to both our kids of color and white kids, though in different ways. If that doesn't seem to work (in my experience, it has been exclusively white parents who think talking about racism is bad), I talk about making sure that their kid learning about racism now will help them to not make a surely unintended error sometime later in life that could live forever on the internet.

Anyway.

Systemic racism is one of those very hard-to-understand things, even for adults, and I'm not a big fan of the idea of "teaching" racism anyway. Starting too broad gives too much room for students to only partially understand. Learning the language of how race operates, I tell my students, is a bit like learning to shoot a gun. It doesn't take long to learn how to do damage with it, but it does take awhile to use it safely, as a tool, to hit what you want to hit. Put another, less gunny way, I want my students to do more than be able to call something racist. I want them to understand and explain why and how racism works.

I start by talking about how white I am. By midyear, it should not come as a surprise that I'm white, but even (or especially) in antiracist circles I've seen too much "I'm white, but not, like, *really* white" kind of talk because it's comforting to anchor any discussion of racism in how you're not, you know, one of *those* white people because of your partner or kids or colleagues or students or friends or music tastes or whatever. I get it. Alas, I am whitey white. I think it's important to own that, to own how it took me a long time to be comfortable saying that, or talking about what being white has meant for me.

In previous schools, I did a lot less of that, but this school has been different. On one of the very first days discussing a more modern text (Jesse Williams's BET Awards speech), a student pointed to a line where Williams talked about white people (which he does only briefly, saying, "Looking at the data . . . we know that police somehow manage to de-escalate, disarm, and not kill white people everyday"). The student said that this mention of white people made him feel immediately like he was being blamed for racism, made it hard to listen to anything else that Williams had to say.

I was so glad this student spoke up. With the number of heads nodding in the room, I was so glad he said something, and it could not have been an easy thing to say. This is actually a moment where being a white dude is pretty helpful, because I've felt those things. When I went to my first antiracism training during my first year of teaching, I resisted it personally, emotionally, and intellectually because it made me feel guilty, because less than a year away from my dad dying, I didn't feel like my life had been easy or easier or anything. It took me a while to come through that, to work through that, but I got there.

To that student, on that day, I named white guilt specifically, and we talked about it a little bit. We went back to the text even, looking for places where Williams was blaming white people and finding none. We talked about "Letter from Birmingham Jail," which more specifically calls out white moderates and discussed what King thought the role of white people was. On reflection, it was more than I had ever really talked about white people in all my years of teaching about race without focusing specifically on white privilege.

It was actually this moment that made me pause before really digging in on ideas like white privilege and systemic racism. I thought maybe it would be a time to explain my own story a little bit, of acknowledging the guilt that comes when you understand how you have benefited from racism, and trying to model how not to get stuck in or run away from it. So I told my class this, the story of what racism has meant for me, the story of my whiteness, starting with my grandpas.

I'm so white that one of my grandpas is named Walter Otto and one is named Ferdinand Herbert. Walt and Ferd.

I'm so white that they were both involved in World War II, both considered fully American as we fought Germany though the last names in my family are names like Rademacher, Hoppe, and Kraus. They both went to college on the GI Bill after the war, both bought their first homes sometime shortly after, both in newly developing suburbs just outside of Milwaukee, the kinds of places that would have been full of people who had traveled that same path to war and then college and then marriage and then their first home. Ferd stayed in that near suburb, moving from a house big enough for the kids to one small and fit for retirement. He worked for a bank or as an accountant. (Or something like that. The Ferd side of the family was never great at talking much.) I know they had enough money, growing up, that they had a boat built just for them, the kind you can sleep in the bottom of, if you need to.

It was the things like that, the extra money and the newish cars and, I guess, a whole-ass boat, that my grown-up dad was angry he didn't have. Dad smoked a lot of weed, got caught doing so in at least one job, and was fired but not arrested. He bounced slowly from sales to selling stuff to a job driving a passenger van, and at each step he saw the world he thought was owed him slipping away.

Walt, however, eventually sold his house in the near suburbs for a nice profit and bought one in the far suburbs. This one was right on a lake, and, at least in the mind's eye of little me, fucking huge. There was even a boathouse with a little motor system that would bring the boat in and out of the water. Writing that, I can still hear that motor perfectly, still smell the oil and gas and lake water of that boathouse.

I'm white enough that it took until many years after all that, many years after Walt and Ferd had died, to understand their story as something a little more complex than an American tale of the life that one gets when they work hard and, you know, more like what happens when you worked hard and got lucky and were white.

Because, here's the thing. That GI Bill that helped them both finish college on the government's dime? That was widely available only to white GIs. And new suburbs with all those new affordable houses for all the new families popping up after the war? The FHA mortgages that built all that were almost exclusively given to white people.

There's a PBS documentary, *Race: The Power of an Illusion,* that I will often show in class shortly after I tell this story. At one point the documentary throws out a statistic that I pause on to discuss, often stopping for a quick lesson on how home equity and generational wealth work: "Of the $120 billion worth of new housing subsidized by the government between 1934 and 1962, less than 2 percent went to nonwhite families." Less than 2 percent. And those families of color able to get the new fancy affordable mortgages at the time were mostly banned from buying houses in those nice new suburbs, either by the cities, the builders, or by individual covenants written into the deed of the home.

This isn't my history scholarship, but it is a piece of our shared national history and is my personal history, the part of my personal history that was absent from the family narrative of our history. My grandpas got their own chunk of that $120 billion, and so did all the houses around them. That money paid for new schools and parks and roads and all the things that make houses worth more every year. They worked hard, yes, harder than I ever have, but their wealth and lifestyles were also subsidized by the federal government in a way that never would have happened if they were Black. That subsidy meant that both my parents inherited money from their parents, and it meant that even at our most brokey-broke, there was always a safety net to catch us.

I'm so white that even when we slept in our winter coats because the heat was off, and even when the phone would get turned off a few times a year, we never felt poor.

I'm so white that my sister is actually named Karen. We're in a family of four kids, a total of five years apart. Growing up, we spent a lot of time at Grandpa Walt's house, swimming in the lake in the summer and having giant Christmases in the winter.

One night, my grandma, Walt's wife, Patricia, was watching the news. There had been a shooting in Milwaukee, they said. She recognized the street behind the reporter, could see the house my pretty-newly-divorced mom was raising the four kids in. So Walt and Pat bought us a house three or four suburbs out down I-94. We paid them rent when we could, which wasn't always. Walt worked his ass off nearly every day of his life to support his ten kids, to give them clothes and food, and what he could build or fix himself, he did. When the grandkids started coming, Walt and Pat would invest a grand for each of us, money that would, when we got to college, help pay for clothes and food and help to finance many of our first big mistakes.

I'm so white, I was named after a major league pitcher famous now for getting elbow surgery. Tommy John. I named my kid one of those white-people names that are quirky enough that there's rarely a keychain at the gas station with their name on it but not so quirky that there aren't other kids with the same name.

I have hope in all the ways that Olive is growing up different from how I did, that even though they are the next chapter in the book of my family, they have a story that is a lot different.

I grew up in Milwaukee, Wisconsin, in the '80s. Ollie is growing up in Minneapolis, Minnesota, in the right now.

From a covert-racism point of view, the baked-in racism of opportunities and barriers and reward for white cultural behaviors makes any difference between the two pretty much a wash. From the point of view of more overt racism, of cultural segregation and family influences, Ollie looks at a much better world.

The first racist thing I remember hearing is my dad calling the NBA "Blacksketball." That sort of mega-witty racial humor permeated Milwaukee when I was growing up. I didn't know anyone who would admit they were racist, but I sure did hear a whole lot of racist jokes (on my dad's side of the family especially). He and his brothers tended to be pretty low-key about their racism, but his brother-in-law Dan was the first person that I heard use the

N-word. This uncle, a nearly always angry man, likely a few drinks in, was sitting in his chair next to the stack of *Playboy* magazines he didn't feel the need to hide when a whole bunch of kids were coming over. I couldn't have been more than eight. He was talking about how dangerous the city was then, and he spat the N-word out of his thin lips, sticking it against my small eyes.

No one said anything, not to him. He hated Black people, sure, but also women, and gays, and kids, and poor people. I tried to stay away from him. Still do. In fact, I can only think of one time that Olive has ever been in the same room as Dan, which was a Christmas dinner when Ollie was about two. I hadn't seen Dan, or really any of my dad's side of the family, for a few years, and was hoping that the introduction of young children and time and common sense would have maybe evened some of these things out.

It wasn't so bad that I started a fight at the dinner table, but it was close many times. Dan made throwaway comments about how emotional women were, or cracked nagging-wife jokes, but the family had grown more adept at layering a conversation quickly on top of things so that everyone could pretend they hadn't been said. Olive was at the far end of the table, being doted on by another aunt and uncle, whose kids were not yet old enough to give them grandkids, but who were obviously more than ready for it to happen.

I figured an argument between me and Dan would be more likely to draw Ollie's ears and attention to him, and so I just did my best the rest of the night to steer them away from the uncle I didn't want to be anywhere near anyway. After that night, we only went to gatherings that we knew Dan wouldn't be around for. I only see him now when he pops up on my brother's Facebook page, where he is often saying some form of very thinly veiled racism or transphobia. He's a miserable, hateful, sad, and scared old man. I don't miss him and am glad that Olive has no idea he even exists.

From third through fifth grade, I went to school at Golda Meir School for the Gifted and Talented in Milwaukee. It was a magnet for students throughout Milwaukee who showed particular academic aptitude or who, like me, had an older brother who was super smart and got in, and they were willing to keep families together.

I was there from 1990–92, the Golden Age of colorblindness. (So much so that we were supposed to call it a "Don't Care If It's Golden, White, Black, Purple, or Polka-Dotted" Age . . . or, wait, the "Is It Golden? I Didn't Even Notice" Age.) My gifted school was very gifted at obsessing about skin color while pretending that it didn't matter and didn't exist. It was also the first place I really started learning about race.

The school had very specific rules whenever awards or rewards were given. First, there was never one winner of anything, there were always two, and those two people could not share a racial or gender identity. The same rule was true with teacher-assigned partners for projects, field trips, and lunchroom seating charts. At that school, at that time, it meant I got to know the Black girls of Golda Meir really well.

I can't argue that this was a bad thing for me. My whole family is white, as were my neighborhood friends (meaning, my one friend, the kid next door who licked his top lip so much that it was always bright red and irritated, and also let his dogs lick the inside of his mouth, but also who had a Nintendo). Anyone who teaches will tell you that these late elementary years are often the ones when students start to self-segregate by race and gender when given the chance, so going to a racially diverse school wasn't going to necessarily mean my world wouldn't have stayed mostly white.

The intention of the practice makes some sense. It does some good stuff but also doesn't really solve any problems. For example, we didn't ever talk about cultural differences and how to understand and accept them. We didn't talk about how race and skin color impacted any of the scientific, literary, or historic things we were learning about.

Often, it was just kinda weird. I was one of a few white boys in a grade with some very high-achieving Black girls. So since they kept winning awards for stuff they earned, I ended up winning a bunch of shit and getting a bunch of certificates that I didn't really deserve.

Ain't that just the way of it?

Still, beyond shoving us together, obviously and repeatedly, in a way that was linked directly to our skin color, the rule was never actually spoken aloud to students, nor was any discussion about skin color had in a meaningful way. There was lots of "all the same on the inside" talk, and nothing about how our experiences or perspectives could be different. For those discussions, for the real beginning of my racial education, I had to wait for recess.

Recess at Golda Meir consisted of two things of equal importance: kickball and arguing about TV. Kickball at Golda was epic. Stories were told about the heroes of years past. (My brother's year had a kid who was nicknamed Tarzan, but only at recess, who would let out his namesake's signature scream whenever he scored. When he was playing, everyone on the playground, teachers included, stopped to watch.) The school and grounds took up a city block in downtown Milwaukee, with tall fences surrounding the playground. A homerun meant clearing the ball over that fence, usually to watch it bounce blocks down the hill we were on top of. By fifth grade, I had a pretty strong leg but only managed to hit the fence twice. On a bounce. No tales were told.

But anyway.

The way I remember it, and it's only been, like, thirty-something years, the only other thing we ever talked about was what we watched on Thursday nights. One group of us watched *The Simpsons* and one group watched *The Cosby Show.* This was decades before we realized how messed up it was to have a white person voice the problematic-anyway Apu and before there was any debate about whether or not we should just burn every episode of *The Cosby Show* from history. Instead, the only thing we argued about was which show was in fact the single greatest show of all time.

Battle lines were drawn along the racial differences we had been told not to notice. White kids watched *The Simpsons,* Black kids watched *Cosby.* I can picture perfectly the place by the side stairs, where buses were loaded, where we stood once, shouting our arguments and disparaging what we assumed the other show was like. (No one was ever willing to take a week off to watch the other.) We almost came to blows.

These other students were my friends, were my classmates and kickball teammates, and yet here they were loving this show that wasn't even a cartoon? I didn't get it. It was the first time I remembered thinking that, huh, maybe there were some differences between white kids and Black kids. Not biological differences or anything, but *The Simpsons* was such a central part of not just my childhood but of the whole culture and humor of my family. When my dad found out that he had emphysema on top of, like, three kinds of cancer, he started his phone call to me saying, "I'm invincible!"—referencing an episode where Mr. Burns finds out that he has so many diseases in his body that they are somehow balancing each other out. It took my little brain a whole lot of work to wrap around the idea of another family gathering around the TV to watch a show starring the pudding guy.

Looking back on those arguments, one of the great failures of our school was that by telling us all the time that everyone was the same, we never really learned to appreciate each other's differences. We had no room or language in our brains to believe that both *The Simpsons* and *The Cosby Show* could be the best show, depending on what you were looking for and who you were watching as. There had to be one, a central truth, and so mainly we just shouted a lot at each other.

Olive's early school experience was very different. Their elementary school was an "international" school that purposefully integrated cultures of its students into its curriculum and climate. The school boasted about the number of language and countries represented by the families in their school (both were more than thirty), and students learned, through exposure and experiences with each other and through school events and intentional planning, that there is power and beauty in diversity. Watching Ollie go to school there, it actually felt a lot less like students being taught and more like students being allowed, like they were naturally aware of and appreciative of the things that made their classmates different from them.

Our liberal pocket of Minneapolis did some reinforcing of those ideas. Though gatherings at our home of groups of friends were often more white than I would like to admit, Ollie spent their childhood going to places, festivals, and performances that not only celebrated other cultures but weren't built specifically for comfort or consumption of white people. As a young person I had few to none of those experiences, struggling now to think of even one thing I may have attended that wasn't serving bratwurst.

Through my young eyes, Milwaukee was an interesting place racially. When I was young, Black activist Michael McGee was threatening to throw burning tires onto the freeway. I remember looking up at overpasses when we drove under them, scanning for Black people who might try to kill me. I remember watching the local news, half Packers updates and summer music festivals, half horror stories of Black violence, and knowing which world was mine.

We grew up in a fairly diverse neighborhood, but the white kids never really played with Black kids. We were taught to be colorblind but also felt the tension of the adults when there were Black people around. We were taught to never say the N-word, but to remain silent in the presence of someone who did.

I could have been a white supremacist then, had I been more impressed by my uncle's anger, had my parents said nothing in the car rides home and away from him. I could have grown into a racist, one of those sinewy, angry white guys who blame Black people for everything, who believe in the goodness of Christian whites while living wholly absent of goodness. If I'd been raised by my uncle instead of my dad, maybe, probably, I would have been.

My dad wasn't racist, though, not capital-R Racist. He was Milwaukee racist, and even then he smoked too much weed to try hard at it. He mellowed, too, as I got older, as he grew less angry at the things he didn't have. He was too young to be a real hippie but still listened to all of their free-love music. Some of that rubbed off on him, and some of that rubbed off on me. Hate always felt like the obviously wrong answer.

My dad died when I was in college, and that still hurts, and this is as negatively as I've ever allowed myself to remember him.

When I moved out of Milwaukee in fifth grade, I spent a couple of years in the suburbs playing the part of the edgy kid, because once upon a time I went to school with Black people. After a few years I stopped being the edgy kid and started being a suburban white kid. I got okay grades, I guess. I spent long weekends at my friend's house listening to him and his older brother make Jew jokes, and making things that blew up in different ways.

In my new school, well, how to best put this . . . ? Every single kid (except the super churchy kids) was a *Simpsons* watcher. My classmates were worried that since I moved from the city I was probably part of a gang, and more than a few of them cornered me at some point to ask what Black people were like, because they had never, not once in their life, actually talked to one. Yes, we were out in farmland, but we were also only a thirty-minute drive from Milwaukee. It took me a few years before I understood that the lack of exposure to people of other cultures and skin colors was considered by many in my town to be a feature, and not a fault, of the life they had chosen.

The district at the time had very few kids of color, and nearly all of them (especially any Black kids) found their way diverted quickly to the "alternative" school in the district, a weird building with no windows, half of which was used to park plow equipment and buses and stuff. We didn't know those kids. We didn't see those kids.

Which is to say this: as soon as I moved away from a school that wasn't all white kids, and that was purposeful (though weirdly secretive) about making kids of different racial identities sit and work with each other, I didn't talk to any people of color my age for eight straight years. By high school, I was dying my hair pink and wearing a spike bracelet and Doc Martens (having signed up at the mail-order "suburban rebellion" club, which sent me a gift basket from Hot Topic and Goodwill every month along with a CD from a band that was anti-"the man"—the first month was only a penny), and on most weekends I would head into Milwaukee to see a punk show of some kind. I would wear antiracist patches and shout along to antiracist songs from antiracist bands in a punk scene that was all white, then drive home to my all-white neighborhood and my all-white school. Although I never really investigated my belief that a majority of people in the world were white and German and kinda Catholic, I never really had it challenged either.

I learned to juggle, played video games for hours, and though I didn't try hard at much, I seemed to be doing fine. One time, two girls asked me out in the same week, though they were the only two girls all year.

Honestly, I was mediocre as fuck.

I went to college in Minneapolis, the biggest city in my region that didn't exist in Illinois (and therefore wouldn't have gotten me kicked out of my family), where one would think things would be a little better. I spent the first couple of years in the bubble of the campus, a place that was much much whiter than the city that surrounded it, but I managed to fall into some friendships with a group of kids from the city and made, at eighteen years old, the first real friends of my life who weren't white. I had a lot to learn.

And so I thank god, or whatever her name is in Minneapolis, for my roommate Stephen, a white dude who was also a DJ and producer and probably the only real-life genius I've ever met. He and I would spend long nights talking about what it meant to be a white dude, often ignoring whole dumb college parties so we could sit in a corner and think about stuff. Stephen taught me, through modeling, what it meant to investigate discomfort rather than run away from it. He loved digging in on stuff, got genuinely excited when he found a piece of his brain or perception or all the rest of that messy goo that didn't work the way he thought it would or wanted it to. He invited me into that process, made it safe to bring up my own shit, and dug through it with me. The only rule of these long talks seemed to be that you couldn't say something just because you felt like you should.

We didn't use words like *privilege* and stuff like that, because Stephen and I hadn't gone to all the workshops and professional development, but the result was very much the same (or probably much much better).

It took me a whole lot of years after that point to realize how rarely white guys do what Stephen did, which is talk about being white and a guy. Stephen gave me a role model and mentor for what it meant to be reflective and aware. Growing up, I didn't really have those role models.

I read Garrison Keillor's *The Book of Guys,* which is a book of stories about how hard and special it is to be a man, but I didn't read it until I was a little older, and I was in a better place, and had a pretty awesome girlfriend who told me it was kinda dumb when I got her to read it.

I could have been an alt-righter. I could have talked publicly in a way that almost sounded smart about how other cultures get to celebrate their heritage, so why not me? And I'm not racist, I'm post-racial. I'm done with the guilt. I would've gotten the dumb haircut. I would've made shitty jokes when it was just me and the guys who I knew "got it," and I would've talked about how people don't understand humor or irony anymore, and anyway free speech and stuff. It would have been easy for me to only know white people my whole life, and to carry ideas of what everyone else was like, and how surely no one was as good as me and my bros.

I hate to think of where I could have gone then, with that community in place, selling the very sweetest smelling lies possible: that I was special, that I was powerful, that my feelings of weakness, awkwardness, ineptitude, rejection were all someone else's fault. That other guys like me had my back as long as I had theirs.

I could have stood in Charlottesville. I could have said I wasn't racist, that I was just "pro–white," that I was a nationalist, that I was only fighting what feminism and affirmative action had unjustly taken from me. That I wasn't racist, but everyone else was racist against me. I could have said it. I could have believed it.

It's terrifying.

I have been, at a few times in my life, the sort of person who becomes an active racist. The frightened, confused child, the teen struggling for meaning and feeling powerless. The white dude who doesn't like feeling guilty when learning about the history of white dudes. The difficult truth is that the path is easy. Embracing white supremacy means never having to say sorry, never having to feel bad. It means empowerment, entitlement.

Olive has never been that person, has never shown even the slightest sign that they are interested in being better or more powerful than anyone else, has shown horror, always, and bewilderment whenever they hear stories of racist violence, of racist policies. They have some growing up to do yet, and as in class, I see it as my duty to mostly let them explore and understand things as they're ready (while giving some explicit instruction when needed). We'll keep making sure Ollie sees examples of joy and art and beauty from all the people in our world, and we'll keep doing our best to keep the sneering racists far away.

Ollie very naturally sees the bad things racism does. They recoil at the idea of hatred; they seem to have no instinct to fear difference. So far, in the ways they can see and understand, they also seem to want to cast off any privileges they may be getting for being a white kid that their classmates or friends or teachers or role models of color are not getting. That kind of privilege and power can be like a drug, can be very hard to see and admit to, much less to let go of. It's also so firmly built into our expectations of what life should be, especially for our white boys, which may be why I've struggled so much trying to address it with white boys, in and out of class.

MARCH

LEMONADE, MOUNTAIN DEW, METH

MY FRIEND NICK AND I WERE TALKING about white boys once. He said, and I'll never forget it, "White boys exist on a spectrum between Mountain Dew and meth." I guess Mountain Dew makes a pretty good stand-in for your average white dude into sports and dick jokes, wielding a perception that the world somehow both belongs to him and owes him something. We're seeing a lot of meth-level dudes showing up these days too, guys who wield their whiteness like a weapon, or like an addiction, destructive and disastrous.

I wrote a piece once about how I'm worried about white boys, about how the level of privilege afforded to us, the violence with which we defend that privilege, has lowered expectations for our behavior. A whole lot of people got real upset. Not exactly "I'm going to kill you" upset, but definitely "Here are all the ways I hope you die" upset. One person said they wished my students would gas me, which I thought was bizarrely specific. The piece was one of questions and concerns. I did not know how to teach a room of white boys about systemic and personal racism without feeling like I was either making it way too hard or way too easy on them. I still don't really know, but I've learned a few things.

During that first year in the new place, I had a group of white boys who were more near the Mountain Dew end of the spectrum. They weren't, like, racist, you know. Not really. They just didn't really care about race and wanted all the talk about it to go away. They were the "It's not that big a deal" set. That time they linked arms across the hallway and physically blocked other kids from getting through them? Not that big a deal. That time one of them walked into a classroom listening to, and singing loudly along to, a song that included the N-word? Not that big a deal.

It did not take me long to garner a reputation in the school as the social justice teacher. It took me much much longer to garner an understanding with many people that being a social justice teacher was a good thing. To the Mountain Dew boys, it meant that I talked about "all that stuff" way too much, took their jokes way too seriously, and made everything too big of a thing. They were too right about this last one. After trying for not nearly long enough to build up some mutual respect and understanding, I, if I'm honest, defaulted to just being a dick to them when they were being obnoxious (which meant when they were too loud and distracting, but also when they were too quiet and not trying). I don't think I've ever yelled someone into inspiration, or to try something new and uncomfortable, but I still try when I'm failing or frustrated.

The more abrasive I got with them, the more they fucked with me. Of course they did.

For example, here's the most middle school teaching story ever. One day, the group of boys was gathered just outside my room, as they tended to be (three of them had lockers right outside my door). I walked by and saw that they were all passing and sharing a big jug of pink lemonade, doing that thing where they held it just over their mouths without touching and trying (and failing) to pour some in their mouth without getting any on their face or the floor. This moment, the moment when I first saw the lemonade, would be the first of many moments of this saga when

I could have just let something go. Nope. I stopped there in the hallway, proclaiming all sorts of nonsense about where and when lemonade was allowed, and distractions to their learning, and by the next day the lemonade had better be gone.

By the next day, there were no fewer than five big-ass things of lemonade being passed around the hallways and brought into classes. Why? I can think of two reasons. One is that lemonade is very good, and another is that I had made it clear that it bothered me.

It should be clear to anyone who spends time thinking about it that there is no way to win an argument about pink lemonade. By engaging in, by actually starting the argument, I had already lost. By continually policing who had it or was hiding it (who I specifically told not to and who had the audacity to ask me why), or who opened my door at the end of the day and put an empty bottle of it just inside the doorway (they may as well have walked right up to me and given me the middle finger), I was playing right into a game where they got to piss me off by doing something that sounded really really dumb in an email home:

> Dear sir or madam, I am writing to inform you that your student has been brazen enough to drink lemonade on multiple occasions even after being asked to please not drink lemonade. I'm sure you're in the middle of your own problems, perhaps worrying about how your parents are getting up there in age, wondering how long they can live alone, or maybe stressing about stretching a paycheck far enough to get both food and electricity in your house. But, hear me out: this lemonade thing is a real, real problem.

It died out eventually, but the tone of the Week of Lemonade continued most of the year. I was losing hard. This group of boys, athletic and smart, genuinely funny in a way that keeps an orbit of kids around them, and also capable of the sort of casual cruelty that keeps those kids from speaking up to them, saw me as an enemy. If I'm honest, I'm not sure the feeling wasn't entirely mutual.

I spent a lot of time that year thinking about their privilege, their hyperprivileged existence growing up white and male in a suburban community designed for their comfort, happiness, and success. I had so much I wanted to teach them but really struggled to get them to hear anything I had to say. I get it, I do, because I was that kid, too, at one point. Maybe not as talented an athlete or as smart a student, but enough that I could hang around those kinds of kids without sticking out too much. I've also seen enough of those boys grow to see the dangers of growing up in a culture where you can do no wrong, where effort is for other kids, where a strict adherence to a narrow set of guidelines for how to look, act, and think is enforced with brutal silence.

So, no, *enemy* isn't the right word. They pissed me off plenty, kept my blood pressure up, but more than anything I worried about them a lot and was bad at showing it. I worried about the damage they were capable of doing to others, of course, and to themselves. I worried, I lost sleep worrying, about how we might be making baby racists, about what they thought the world owed them, and what they may do when any of those things was denied. We know the grown-up monster versions of protected and powerful white men are everywhere, and they have to come from somewhere. I knew these boys were good, were not that, would never be that, but I worried.

Near the end of the year, finally, I made some decent moves. I had really given up on salvaging my relationship with this particular group of boys. It happens. It's not great, but it happens. However, I knew that after they went off to high school, I was quite likely to see groups much like them year after year in this school, and they all deserved better from me. So I asked them to join me for lunch, told them they weren't required to join me, and I'd get it if they didn't, but that I wanted to hear about how their year went. They didn't seem overly enthusiastic. I offered to order pizza. They promised to be there.

I learned so much, and so many things I should have already known. Once I shut up, they told me about how they felt like they were always getting in trouble for little dumb stuff, which made them care less about everything else. They admitted to not trying very hard in my class as a result and were sorry about it. We laughed a lot about the lemonade thing once I admitted I had lost my mind over nothing.

Boiling it down, what was their biggest issue? They, the loudest group in the school, felt no one was willing to listen to them, and they were right. I knew this. I knew that listening was the most powerful thing, especially with students who are struggling or who I'm struggling with. So why didn't I see it here? I think it's because they were white kids. Because I had spent a decade building up a belief that justice is more important than white feelings (it is), because I didn't want any of these boys to grow up to be my racist uncle (they won't), I demanded their empathy instead of giving it space to develop, modeling my own only toward groups that did not look like them.

I fucked up.

Eighth grade boys are not grownups on the internet. I know that. I think I knew that, but I spend a lot of time swimming in the wokeness Twitter method of expecting white people who show up to do their own work, to have spent some of their time becoming grown people thinking about race in the world (totally a good expectation for adults). It had seeped into my practice as a teacher (where I worked with young people). Not only was it unfair to treat my students like that, it pushed them further away from the work I hoped they would do.

I had a similar talk that year with another group of boys, a group that had the contents of a group text shared with some of their classmates. That chat included jokes about being racist and jokes about race. When they were called on it, they were defensive, defensive to the point of shutting down or shouting at me, up until I told them that I was also once a total dipshit.

When I was an eighth grader, I had hair down to my shoulders and wore the same green flannel almost every day. Kurt Cobain was my hero, and during our eighth grade dance I requested a moment of silence for him (he had died more than a year before). I also made and laughed at jokes about domestic violence, about gay people, about Helen Keller and dead babies, and, I'm sure (though my brain refuses to remember this specifically), about race. The point of the jokes was their absurdity, their offensiveness, playing with a power I didn't understand. I likely don't need to explain the appeal of bad jokes, because I bet nearly everyone reading this knows exactly what I'm talking about. A lot of us made those kinds of jokes growing up. We just got lucky and grew up before the internet.

In ways, pieces of that type of humor are still my favorite. I still love jokes that shock people, still love saying the worst thing that comes to my mind. I would never joke about any of those specific kinds of things anymore, the attacks on people already marginalized and regularly dehumanized. I don't find trauma funny, but the essential blueprint of shock humor is still there. I explained a lot of that to the group-text boys and tried to impart a lesson about knowing your audience and assuming a lack of privacy.

They got it, they get it. Not a one of them wanted to spend time again with an adult reading, word for word, jokes they had texted with their friends. But before that meeting ended, one of the students added a piece to the conversation that I hadn't considered. This was the year after Philando Castille was killed by a member of their town's police department, the year after their seventh grade experience was defined by racial tension in the school, by the sorts of harm and offense and mistakes that twelve-year-olds make when trying to wrestle with issues like privilege and bias and systemic racism that many adults can't talk about with any comfort or confidence. It was many complex things that were to be summarized neatly in the words of the now eighth grade boy: "We got called racist all year."

They felt called out and apart, again and again, for being white. My guess is that no one intended to do so, but I think many white people can identify with that feeling when they first started talking about race, the sort of guilt whenever anyone says "white people," the feeling of being blamed. For many of us, it's the first time we've felt the discomfort of being referred to as a member of a racial group, and we find the experience to be icky. Or, as this one boy was explaining to me, it feels like you're being called racist, and it sucks. So, he explained, they started joking about it on their group text, about being racists and making racial jokes, as a way to "sort of let off steam." Their days were full of heavy conversations, and this was a way to lift some of that weight, however briefly, with a group of people who were sharing that experience with them.

I explained the phrase *gallows humor*, talked about the jokes my brothers and sister made with each other in the weeks immediately following our dad's death. He agreed that it felt very much like that. Does the Gallows Humor Defense excuse the harm their jokes had caused? It does not. Does it explain or excuse every racist joke made by young white men? No. Absolutely no. But it's a piece worth understanding.

I don't think the bad jokes of my eighth grade self had anything to do with the tension of existing as a white male struggling to understand race and racism, not because I was past these things but because I hadn't even shown up yet to that conversation. For me, as a young kid who got away with just about everything he did, whose long hair was enough to attract the attention of a few girls looking for a bad boy in a target-deficient environment, I was terrified of absolutely everything about the world, and humor was the main way I found to pretend that I was not.

I was scared of girls, that they wouldn't like me, or that they would. That they would tease me, however lightheartedly, and expose me for the awkward fraud I was. I was scared of other boys, that they were stronger or faster than I was, obviously much much better looking than I was, and more talented at things that were more interesting. I was scared of everything, and scared, above all else, that my fear would somehow show through.

My understanding now, achieved through a process referred to by most psychologists and sociologists, I believe, as "taking your head out of your ass," is that I had it easier than just about everyone. To be white, straight, and a cisgender male in middle school means that a good portion of my awkward growth came at the expense of others, not as the victim. I was, and am, "wealth" and "good looks" away from checking every box on the privilege card. Something of the expectations of us white boys to be leaders and to be physically strong and emotionally restricted makes many of us, made me, feel scared and powerless about not stacking up, made me search for and cling to anything that made me feel powerful.

Thank god I didn't have the internet.

I mean, I'm not saying the internet is inherently a bad thing. For the most part, I think our young people are the most culturally literate generation in history in large part because of how easy it is for them to access different people and ideas. Olive spends enough time on the internet that it can claim them as a dependent on its, you know, internet taxes. For the past year or two, we've also done very little to monitor or direct that time. So far, they have come to us when someone is swearing too much or when a friend is being mean or, a few times, when they worry they may have accidentally bought a bunch of things inside of some game they were playing. Left on their own, they have found art and music tutorials and communities of young animators and game creators.

One weekend they spent nearly every waking hour in their room on the computer. I had a cold and Becca was working a lot, and we sort of gave up on being decent parents for a few days and figured one weekend of watching a bunch of stupid YouTubers making fart cannons or whatever would be fine. On Sunday night they showed us that they'd been working on a game competition as part of a small community online. Some of the older programmers had been around to answer specific questions about coding or modeling, and some of Ollie's other friends had helped beta-test. The game Ollie made was called Heckin' Pupper, and players assumed the role of the Devil trying to pick the perfect dog as a new pet. Ollie also did all the art for the game, drawing lots of different dogs to choose from, and writing witty descriptions and absurd narration for the game.

Beyond that, Ollie has found nonbinary heroes in art and animation, has seen and interacted with kids around the world doing cool stuff and being cool people, has gathered some role models who are not white, not straight, not American, not Christian, who don't look or talk or act like them or their immediate family. The internet has a whole lot of ideas about just about everything, so Ollie is learning to hear from lots of different people, take the pieces that make the most sense, and make up their own mind about how they feel. The plurality of voices means Ollie doesn't rely on just one or two (certainly not mine) to tell them what to think or feel.

NON-BINARY

The internet can be awesome when the person using it is awesome. At times in my life I was not awesome. I was scared and lonely and not particularly talented at anything. Thank god I didn't have the internet.

I didn't have 4chan or 8chan or Reddit. I didn't have gaming communities of other mediocre-ass white dudes who read too little and jacked off too much. Guys who were, like me, not doing anything special and were still annoyed that we weren't being treated like we were.

I didn't have internet jokes and frog memes and Facebook groups to share the jokes I shared with friends, those jokes that felt powerful because they were so offensive. I didn't have the pushback to those jokes, people telling me, "You, young idiot, have to decide if you are either a racist who thinks that's funny or a good person who doesn't." Social Justice Twitter would have just confirmed for me what the assholes with the Nazi haircuts were telling me on their internet shows, that other people just don't get me, that they want to take things from me, that PC culture is trying to keep me from being a real man. Those scary Nazi assholes know exactly the sort of scared boys they are targeting.

I do have those white boys in my room too. White boys who aren't the super popular loud ones making big dumb mistakes getting slaps on the hand or pats on the back for it. There're also the quiet white boys, the ones with one or two quiet white boy friends. These boys have become recently more interested in Russia once everyone else was blaming them for election interference. When they are allowed to choose topics for projects in my class, they have chosen proto-fascist groups from Eastern Europe, or arguing that the gender wage gap isn't real or why feminism is bad. They watch PragerU videos and cite Ben Shapiro or Steven Crowder.

I get it. To an extent, anyway, I get it. All those dudes do a pretty good impression of what intelligence can sound like, and they do it while affirming that everything out there that makes white guys feel bad is obviously wrong and stupid. There were times in my youth I would have found it all very appealing.

And look, I'm not conservative. I have never voted for a single Republican and can't imagine a scenario that I would (especially once 2000 McCain became 2010 McCain, and you know, he probably won't be running again because he's pretty dead now). That said, I don't care if these kids, if any kids, grow up to be conservative. I do care if they are racist. I do care if they are homophobic. I care if they get pulled into hateful ideologies because they are scared eighth grade boys looking for any way to feel powerful.

I'm not nearly so confident in my own beliefs that I want to pass them down to anyone. What I would like to do is give my students the skills to build up their beliefs on their own, and to be thoughtful while they do it.

My goals are the same for Olive. The story of my own whiteness is one that I, like it or not, am handing off to my kid. My grandfather came of age during the creation of white suburbia. My dad was still a teenager during the Civil Rights era, and I was a kid raised on colorblindness. I've learned to understand privilege and am part of a whole generation who seems very happy with themselves when we are able to name our own privilege whenever possible without really doing anything about it.

I can hope Ollie becomes a tear-this-shit-apart antiracist radical, but I don't even know what that would or should look like for the next generation. I can trust in them, though, trust that they will take the best information we have and do what is right to make things better.

APRIL

SEX ED

THE WORST THING ABOUT THIRD GRADE is knowing that you are mere tens of millions of seconds away from your child being in middle school. I teach middle school, of course, and love middle schoolers. Still, I am not and may never be ready for the hormones, friend drama, and shatteringly awkward flirting of middle school to be in my house.

But right now Ollie is eight, so why would I be thinking about sex ed? Because, in our house some form of sex ed started at a very young age. Young kids need to understand their bodies, so there was some of that, and they have questions about how babies are made, so there was some of that.

Most of Ollie's sex ed so far has fallen to Becca. Not because I'm uncomfortable talking about those things, but for the same reason that I am unworried in general about the kinds of sex ed that Ollie will eventually get (or not) in school and read (hopefully in well-researched, inclusive websites but probably also through memes and horrifically uninformed posts) online. Ollie's mom is a sex therapist. Before she was a therapist, she spent about a decade as a sex educator and wrote a great book that mixed those two things. (It's basically an "everything you need to understand about sex as a professional and how to talk about it with a client/patient in a professional way" manual. It's a goddamn masterwork.) Basically, if Ollie has any questions about sex at any point in their lives,

I'm convinced that Becca is among the top two or three people in the country to ask.

Also, sometimes when I tell people that my wife is a sex therapist, they give me this goofy smile and say, "Oooh, lucky you, that must be fun."

They are correct.

Ollie knows they have a super smart mom. About a month ago, we were driving home from a summer camp that either involved lots of dogs or lots of swords (it's been a weird summer), and Ollie was wondering if Becca would be home that night. As a therapist, Becca spends a few evenings a week seeing clients and on those days generally only gets to see Ollie for a few hours in the morning before school and then peek in on sleeping Ollie when she gets home. "Yeah, Mom should be home when we get there. Why?"

"Oh, I just have some questions about gender and sexuality and stuff." The car is where we get a lot of our deeper questions from Olive. On the way to camp, we had talked about how World War II started, the rise and responsibilities of the United States as a global power after the war, and also took a sharp left turn (as these conversations often do) to talk about the philosophical differences between vegans and vegetarians.

"Well, you can wait for Mom, of course, but you can also ask me. I know some about that stuff, too."

"Dad," they responded, exasperated, "I've been talking to Mom about it for awhile, so I already know everything you know. I want to learn some new stuff about it."

And that was the first time I made Olive walk home.

My own role in sex ed for Olive (since obviously I have no knowledge to add to the subject) was helping to model consent from an early age. With Ollie, and with my nieces and nephews, I often play the role of the roughhouser. I'm the adult who will toss them high in the air into a pool or hang them upside-down walking into a restaurant. I'm also often the tickle monster, who will chase and be chased with threats of tickles.

Pretty standard stuff.

One thing I make sure to do with any kid is make sure I'm asking before I do those things and not make a joke out of not listening when they say no or say stop. With my nephew, this means he will often yell, "No, don't tickle me!" and I'll say, "Okay," and put my arms down, and then he'll see that I mean it and yell, "Tickle me!"

Again, pretty standard. I'm hoping it normalizes control over their own bodies. For the same reason, we try to jump in at the end of events and ask Ollie if they want to hug people goodbye before anyone demands a hug and never pressure them to do it if they don't want to. I know, it's just hugs and tickles, but it feels like the right lessons for the ages of the kids, and I know Becca and I both believe that understanding bodies and sex and gender and all that is important enough that we don't want to leave it to chance and stupid dirty jokes.

My own education in the realm of sexuality began with one such stupid dirty joke.

There's this place somewhere in Wisconsin, a Jewish summer camp with a few big cabins, a big meeting and eating hall, and a pond with a snapping turtle large enough to eat a human. That's how I remember it anyway, but, then, I was pretty young. My elementary school took students there in fourth grade for a two-night camping thing every year. I went every year for a while because my mom taught at the school and would go along to chaperone. This was the place I learned to play Capture the Flag, where I learned it was a bad idea to try to pee in the woods while lying down hiding during Capture the Flag (no matter how bad you have to go), where I learned to build a fire, and where I learned that some people have penises that can go in other people's vaginas.

I was in second grade, walking with a group of fourth graders through the woods for night games, and one was telling a dirty joke.

One of the other kids stopped him because I was there: I was two years younger, and my mom was a teacher. Somewhere in the woods, my older brother was hiding or running or something with the rest of his grade. I kinda had to pee but was sure I could hold it until after the game.

"Nah, he's okay with jokes. Right?"

Yup. Totally okay. "Yeah. Right."

The joke centered around a young man whose name was Johnny Deeper. Johnny Deeper. This was not a subtle or clever joke, in case you are wondering. It is, however, the first joke like it that I ever heard and is seared deeply into my brain, forming a sort of bedrock on which other memories have been built. The joke ended, after many twists and turns, with Johnny's father finding him with a woman in his bedroom and yelling his son's name. Johnny answered, "I'm trying, Dad!"

Again, this was not a clever joke.

The fourth graders laughed and laughed. A whistle blew, signaling to us that we only had two minutes left to hide. I really had to pee now and hoped the game wouldn't take too long.

For many, too many years, this joke was the extent of my sex education. Well, the joke, and that one time the neighbor kid and I walked in on his dad watching porn, the memory of which I can only describe as *distressing*.

Lord knows what I thought sex was at that point.

In middle school we did some sex ed, but I paid as much attention to that as I did to everything else in middle school. It was sex ed, I remember, that was interrupted so we could all watch the O.J. verdict on a TV cart rolled to the front of the room.

Growing up, I remember three specific lessons about women and relationships from my dad. The first two were both bedrock memories, ones where I can remember just where I was standing or sitting, the lighting in the rooms, what was happening around us, but couldn't really tell you how old I was except that I was too young to remember how old I was. For all these moments, my dad had adopted a sort of dad-advice voice that I only heard him break out one other time in my childhood, which was to give eight-ish-year-old-me advice on drugs (wait until college, then do whatever you want, but no needles).

The first time Dad talked to me about women, we were sitting on our scratchy brown-and-tan couch watching the Packers lose and trying to be excited about Don "Majik Man" Majkowski (with the Heart song playing at least once a game). During a commercial break, women in bikinis danced in the ways that women in bikinis dance when selling beer. There was an awkward silence before my dad looked down at me and said, "Real women don't look like that." I didn't gather that he thought real women looked bad or anything, just not like the women on TV. There was another awkward silence, then the game was back on.

The second time was just inside the front door. I had come in from playing with the new He-Man Castle Grayskull a neighbor kid got. My dad was playing with his stereo in the room off to the left, which is something he often did when trying to calm himself down. "Tom," he said, in that voice, "I don't regret having you or the other kids, but getting married was the biggest mistake I've ever made." I had no idea how to respond to that.

Shocking no one, my parents divorced soon after.

Dad stayed away from relationship advice for many many years after that until the day he drove me up for my freshman year of college. We took stuff up elevators in industrial laundry carts stamped on the side with the name of my dorm. We went out for lunch and shakes at the place where all the parents took their kids out for lunch and shakes when they came to visit, and then sat in his car outside of the dorm for a minute before he started his five-hour drive home.

"Tom," he said, his voice like a tuning fork that buzzed those other memories awake again in my head, "I just want to say, you know . . ." He stared out the windshield, watching as another family pushed one of those same carts from their minivan to the sidewalk. "College is a crazy time. You're probably going to go to parties, and those parties are probably going to get wild, and . . . well . . . I just want to tell you, that if you have the chance to have a three-way, take it, or you'll regret it for the rest of your life."

He gave me a little half-hug, and off I went to face the world with far, far more questions than answers.

Some twenty or so years since school stopped for the O.J. verdict, my eighth graders came to my class after health. It was sex ed time, so I was expecting some sex ed giggles, but there were none.

"Sex ed is dumb," they said. "Super boring," they said. "Killing my soul," one particularly melodramatic student said, banging her fist against her forehead. "It's the worst."

This, I thought, *this is proof that smartphones have, finally, ruined the brains of young people.* When sex isn't exciting enough, we may as well burn the whole damn thing down.

"How could sex ed be dumb?" I asked.

"Because," she said, now rolling her forehead against her desk like it was a cold pack, "they wouldn't even talk about sex."

"Huh?"

"They just said not to."

"Oh."

"They just said good people didn't have sex, and we shouldn't be bad people."

"Seriously?"

"Seriously."

Hands went up. Many hands. Students disappointed in their previous class remembered that I am easily distracted by random questions and will entertain just about any conversation my students want to have.

"Like, okay. Rad. Rad. RAD. Do you think it makes someone a crappy person if they have sex before marriage?"

Wait. What the fuck happened in that class? I mean, you probably know what happened in that class. They were teaching abstinence-only sex education in an era after the invention of color television. It hadn't occurred to me this could possibly still be a thing, but this was the group that always got invited in by my district, and it seemed a lot of the people who had until recently been in charge were happy to leave well enough alone.

The phy ed teachers also taught health and were trying to get things switched. I was the appalled English teacher trying not to look like the teacher who cares too much about sex ed (while knowing that that exact stigma is the root cause of why so much sex ed sucks in our country). Because I'm an English teacher, sex ed doesn't really fall under my umbrella, but that doesn't mean I haven't snuck some in here or there (cue my brain replaying the Johnny Deeper joke for the four millionth time because of the phrasing there).

For the first chunk of my teaching, I taught *Romeo and Juliet* to eighth graders. Beyond opportunities to play with Nerf swords and make fun of Leonardo DiCaprio, the play offered us chances to talk about a whole lot of sex. I started every year by explaining in exacting detail all the different dick jokes in the opening scene. In my first year, my principal walked in mid-lesson, and the kids just about lost their damn minds. As we read through the scene, now with the cryptic Elizabethan English revealed to be not unlike a

Family Guy episode, students were red-faced and struggling to get their lines out through peels of laughter.

Eventually, the principal stood and raised his hand. "All right," he stopped us, "I'm missing something here. Anyone want to clue me in?" And of course one kid did, because there's always that one kid who will.

"Well," he stood as well, making full eye contact with the man who could fire me at any moment for any reason, "when the one guy said, ''Tis known I am a pretty piece of flesh,' he's pretty much saying, 'I have a great penis.'" The principal looked from the student to me. I confirmed, yep, the kid is right. The kid, however, was not done. "And when his friend replies and says he is a 'poor john,' he is saying that everyone knows his friend's penis is dried and shriveled up like a salted herring."

My principal, my boss, this impressive and intimidating man who had not observed in my classroom before this day, looked at me again, like, "There is no way you are doing this right now."

But what could I do? The kid was right. Not only that, the lesson set up this incredible teachable moment about why Shakespeare would have started his play off with two losers making dick jokes. They work. They worked then, they work now. Dicks are funny, dick jokes are funny, and a room full of eighth graders are about as hard to entertain as the crowd of drunk assholes that Shakespeare was writing for. I was just about to explain that all, but the principal left. Just walked out, two beats of awkward silence after a student in my class told him about a shriveled penis. He walked out, my class laughed even harder, and I tried to laugh along with them while cold sweat formed on the back of my neck.

The principal came by again at the end of the day. I was ready to throw myself at his feet and ask for forgiveness. I was ready to explain that he had only seen one moment and not the context of the lesson. I was ready to talk about how I was on cold medicine and just wasn't myself today. I was ready to call the coffee shop I worked at before teaching and ask if they would take me back. But then this thing happened. My principal, a man with no reason not to, trusted me to teach, trusted my intentions.

"I always hated Shakespeare," he said. "But you had a room full of eighth graders hanging on every word of that play today."

Yep.

"I don't care what you did to get them there. If your kids are always that engaged when I walk by, you are doing a great job."

How's that for principaling? Good things happen when we trust teachers to take risks. My principal encouraged me to keep going, and that empowered me to talk about any other issues the play raised. So what if we were talking about dirty jokes all day? We were reading Shakespeare, which is what smart people do.

I mean, sure, dick jokes aren't sex ed, but we did get there. Jokes about maidenheads led to clearing up lots of misconceptions and myths about the hymen. Discussions about the real age of the young lovers led to talk about how often bodies are ready to have babies well before people often are.

None of this was really sex ed either, though. Still, the way we treat sex and bodies and consent in our classrooms is important all the time, not just during a specific sex ed class. It's easy, especially while reading a lot of books often taught in schools, to support ideas that minimize women and women's pleasure, to treat consent as something that can be earned through money or power, and to enforce an idea that women are good for little more than to look good and have sex with complicated and problematic men.

Like so many other things, there is no neutral position to take on sexuality and gender in your classroom. As a teacher, through what and how you teach, through conversations with and around students, through policies you enforce (or not), you will send messages about bodies and gender and consent. So it's very worth being careful about what those messages are.

One year, in a building where I taught, a young woman was being disciplined by a behavior dean. He was walking her to his office and she said, quite clearly, that she didn't feel comfortable being in his office with him. He told her that she had to go anyway. Luckily, her friends saw it, came to me, and I went and sat with her in the office, but still. This is a version of something that happens all the time in schools, whether or not the student is able to so clearly express their discomfort at the time.

I had never thought of the way our control of student behavior takes away agency over their bodies until I talked with Becca about why this situation seemed so off. She pointed out how we often control students by telling them where and how to sit, when to go to the bathroom, how to walk, where to be, and who to be near. Whether we are trying or not, we're sending messages to students about their bodies all the time.

What do the standard texts in our schools tell our students about love and relationships and bodies? I've been wracking my brain about this for days, going through the texts that I've taught, that are taught in buildings where I've worked, that I was handed when I was in school. I'm struggling to find examples of healthy romantic relationships. At first, I was struggling to think of examples of any real relationships in books, which seemed to be by design. I imagine that we are more terrified of addressing romance, most especially sexual romance, in classrooms. So no love or healthy communication anywhere in the canon that I could think of, but I could think of tons of books and stories that carried rape scenes in their pages or that alluded to sexual assault or molestation. Tons more had scenes of physical abuse of children and partners. But none, none that I could think of, suggested that sex is something that people find to be enjoyable when done in a healthy, consensual way.

Seriously, the most sex-positive piece of literature I've taught that is typical in schools was *Romeo and Juliet,* and they get married after knowing each other for, like, a day, speak a full five minutes to each other, and then both commit suicide. Not a good model.

The most successful sex ed program I've ever been a part of was also the easiest to plan. For the first part of the day we invited in some professional sex educators from a local clinic. We have a few in our area, and they all seem pretty equally awesome. I bet you have some in your area who are great too, who will likely come to your school for free (but you absolutely should pay if you can) and will carry with them two key strengths. First, they know what they are talking about. Second, they are not a school employee, so if they do something awful like telling the full truth about something, it's easy to say, "We will not invite them back" to the angry whoever.

Anyway, they came in the morning. They had charts and talked a lot about plumbing and some about the unfortunates that are out there and how to avoid them, and also where and how they could, even as young people, get access to stuff or care or information they might need. These educators, wonderful and underpaid as they are, are also not superstar presenters always. Sometimes they're just super big sex-nerds who have this job for right now. That's cool. Super big sex-nerds are awesome. They come in, an educator who doesn't know my kids, who may not have a natural command of a room of twelve-year-olds, who is just straight-up lecturing and making them listen while using every word they aren't supposed to admit to thinking about, and who is in all these ways set up for failure.

And then, guess what? They don't fail.

We have cornered these young, unpracticed humans with as many as sixty middle school students, students who had been for months making us, us super professional, totally-know-what-we're-doing teachers lose our goddamn minds, and these sex educators have the students hanging on their every word.

Why?

Because they want to know! Because they want to be safe! Because they think about sex all the fucking time but don't really know anything about it!

So the mornings were a good and necessary thing.

In the afternoon we switched it up a bit. We combined some classes so we could have our science teacher and me together with the kids. She was the biology expert, where I, the humanities teacher, was there to answer questions from a societal/emotional standpoint. We both know a good amount, and both are honest enough to say so when we don't, but, really, we were both there because we were adults who were willing to be super honest and who had, generally speaking, the trust of our students.

Also, we're both super fucking funny. So, you know, that was also a plus.

We had students write down questions randomly and hand them in, then spent the hour reading and answering them as best as we could. Students asked about how to say no to sex and how to say yes to it. I remember two questions best. One student asked about how much it was supposed to hurt when you had sex for the first time. Our science teacher took that one.

"It's not," she said. "It's not supposed to hurt, and anyone telling you otherwise is not to be trusted."

Yes, she continued to explain, there can be some discomfort sometimes and whatever, and everyone's body is different and reacts differently and all of those things, but the main message she wanted to give them, a message nearly never given to young people, was this: "Sex is not supposed to hurt. Sex is supposed to feel good. If it doesn't feel good, you should stop and figure it out." She said that one part—the "sex is supposed to feel good" part—really loudly. She repeated it, I'm pretty sure.

We aren't supposed to tell young people that. How fucked up is that? If we don't tell them, assure them that sex is supposed to feel good, if we scare the shit out of them about how dangerous and painful sex is, then they won't expect healthy, positive experiences, and they won't know how and when to ask for help if they need it. They should. We should want that for them.

As we read private questions and answered them, a fun thing happened. Students started raising their hands. They realized, I think, that everyone in the room had questions about sex. Some were funny, and that's okay, and some showed how scared or excited they were, or how they were both things, and that was okay, too.

One student raised his hand high, the sort of hand raising that threatens to pull someone completely from their seat. It took me a moment to register that this student, Noah, had a real, legitimate question to ask. He had a look in his eye, a curiosity, I had very rarely seen from him in any time that he wasn't researching marijuana online for every project he was allowed to pick his topic for.

"Noah."

"Yeah, I have a question."

So rare was this behavior for him that he didn't quite recognize how it worked, that having his hand raised and having his name called carried with it an assumption of a question.

"Shoot."

"What's the clitoris for?"

Pause for giggles. Right? All the giggles from the sixty or so eighth graders and the mention of the clitoris?

Wrong. Dead quiet. It wasn't just Noah. Everyone wanted to

know what the clitoris was for. Like a paragraph, they had always been told it was important, but never been told what it did.

I looked to my colleague, the biology-master-scientist, owner of a clitoris, to answer the question, but she bounced it back, saying, "Nope, I already said that sex felt good. You're up."

See? We're funny. She's funny anyway.

Anyway.

"Okay. So you did the diagrams today, right?"

Noah nodded, confidently.

"So you know right about where the clitoris is?"

Noah nodded, slightly less confidently.

"So what's it for? It doesn't, like, DO anything. It is essentially a bundle of nerves, some external and some internal, so it can feel things. It is, for many people who have them, one of the main ways that sex feels good. In fact, it is the only organ in the human body whose sole purpose is to create pleasure. That's what it does."

Noah nodded, thoughtfully, then looked up, excited, and shouted, "All right, Clitoris!"

Noah began to clap.

Noah's table began to clap with him, and the applause spread quickly to every table in the room. Noah and a few other students were then standing and applauding.

A standing ovation, for the clitoris.

I nearly ran to the band room to grab a microphone, bring it back to my room, and then drop it.

This is the kind of sex ed I want Olive to have. There should be ample places to ask questions and have them answered without shame. There should be at the very least equal attention paid to things like communication and healthy relationships as there is to all the physical body stuff, and every single person making their way through this planet should be having regular and meaningful conversations and lessons about consent.

If the world has taught us anything over the past few years, if thousands of brave women have taught anything to anyone who is listening, it's that there's not just a few bad apples, not just a few bad guys. There is seismic change needed in how we treat sex and sex ed in this country, and my guess is that there are very very few of us who could say that we personally couldn't do better.

Because here's the thing. I'm generally a guy who knows about this stuff. I'm generally a guy who identifies as a feminist, as a social justice warrior, as a genuinely good person.

But, then, also. Let me tell you about the worst thing I've ever done, even though I don't want to. Even though I didn't mean to, there is a person out there for whom I am their worst person. There was a time that I was single and dating and really fucked up and didn't ask the right questions or listen for the right answers.

I hate this story, and it's impossible to tell. Much of it isn't my story to tell, and I also don't want any bit of it to feel like rationalization.

We were dating, and we were physical. At the time, I was terrible at communication, and even as we grew closer and knew each other better, I never got really good at having the conversations we should have been having. I thought, I think, that liking and caring about each other was enough. I knew about consent. It was asked for and given. I didn't know about enthusiastic consent. I didn't know how even a yes could be not enough.

She told me so, explained it to me a year or so after, made me promise to learn to be better, then asked that I not contact her. That was two decades ago now, and I haven't. I have wanted to, many times. I've wanted to tell her about how much I've done to understand what went wrong and how awful I've felt and everything, but

I know that I want to connect so that I will feel better, and that I told her I wouldn't reach out, and that if she wanted to find me I am findable.

I feel like shit about this whole thing, still think about it a lot, but I bet it's not as bad as it made her feel. I bet it's not as often as she thinks about it. I hope that's not true for her. I'm the one who should still be thinking about it, should be thinking hard about what went wrong, about how, even while considering myself to be a thoughtful, caring, feminist ally, I made someone feel unsafe.

I've worked up to a few takeaways. The biggest has to do with understanding that it is my job to understand the power dynamics, which could be based on age or experience or body size or location or any number of things. The biggest takeaway, though, the one I am embarrassed to have not always understood, is that if you keep going till you hear no, it's likely you've already gone too far. There are many good reasons why people may be scared to say no, which is why relying on that one word to cover every kind of consent is not enough.

It is ultimately my responsibility that I once made another person feel bad. It is my responsibility to make sure I never do that again. But also, also, it can be my work to try to keep others from making the same sorts of mistakes. Consent is easy, except it's incredibly messy, and you can hurt someone without intending to and it will still be your fault.

These are the sorts of lessons we never seem to talk about during sex ed, but hey, do you want to know a secret? We really should.

During my first year in the suburbs, we were running into problem after problem with our eighth grade boys. It started as just a general amount of privilege wielding, assuming they could simultaneously not give a fuck, mess around all the time, and be rewarded as great students and leaders. And then, you know, spring happened, and all their attention turned to the young women in their grade. Or, I dunno, I really don't want to blame seasons or hormones or whatever. They were being jerks, and also it was spring.

We found out about some text threads through the highly sophisticated means of investigation that teachers usually find things out, meaning that someone came and told us. It turned out that in one group text boys were mining the Instagram accounts of their female classmates and sharing any pictures that they may have posted in swimsuits or that they found otherwise appealing. Another group of boys had been secretly taking pictures of their female classmates in class or in the hallways. I don't know which is worse. They both make me ill and also fucking angry.

This is where having good teammates comes in really handy. The eighth grade science teacher Kristine was with me in dealing with a lot of these things. There were parent calls and consequences, but so much of it seemed bigger than all that, bigger than the few names we had found for sure. It felt cultural.

We had all these days coming up, the days after testing where you can't really do anything but you can't really do nothing. Kristine and I talked with some of the leaders of the grade, young women who heard some of what was going on and were disgusted and angry and wanted us to do something. We let them in on the planning and preparation as much as they wanted to be and came up with a really great half-day thing. What they really wanted, what they really felt they needed, was space for the female members of the grade to talk and learn together about how to stick together and speak up about cultural misogyny.

This meant splitting kids up by gender, which also felt really fucked up. In 157,680,000 seconds, which group would Olive join?

How uncomfortable would they be even being asked to join? We did have a few kids that year who were either transitioning or questioning their gender. We had a teacher with a good relationship with each talk to them beforehand, let them know what was happening in each group, let them pick wherever they wanted to go. It wasn't perfect. I don't feel good about it. But also the girls asked for and really needed and loved that space.

We invited Abby Honold in. She's a sexual assault survivor and activist who now gives talks about bystander interventions and rape culture and who speaks honestly and brutally and thoughtfully about her own experiences. We had her scheduled for forty-five minutes in the auditorium with the eighth grade girls. They went two hours until we needed to cut them off. I wasn't with them; I was with the boys watching the film *The Mask You Live In* and discussing masculinity and the messages we get about what it means to be a man.

Both groups met outside for the last half-hour of the day for popsicles, because that's how middle school goes sometimes. A group of a few girls and boys came up to me after ten minutes. They had been talking. They demanded that the groups get to switch during the next week and do the other thing. So, you know, we did.

I don't know. I don't know what we accomplished, but it felt a little like we had helped to divert a river, however little, at a critical point. Before they all went to high school, we had had meaningful conversations about consent, about disruption. We named objectification and misogyny and gave our students tools to continue to see and name it.

The next year we added to the process. Abby came back, though this time speaking to the whole grade at once. (We talked with as many students as we could: all said they felt comfortable as a full group and wanted to hear what everyone said.) Our phy ed/health teacher came to us with the idea to make a full-grade, weeklong unit around consent and healthy relationships. The whole team dove in, and students got classes on anatomy, consent, on safer sex and how to communicate with partners. One day I gave a whole lesson on how to hear the word *no* without becoming defensive or offensive, and also particularly how, instead of waiting to hear a no before stopping, to think about all the reasons that someone may not be comfortable saying that and instead look for enthusiastic yesses.

When the year ended and summer hit, our school community was rocked by multiple allegations of sexual misconduct from high school staff (or allowed by high school staff). The allegations were from times before I was in the school, from students whom I never taught, but it made me worried all over again that we weren't doing enough. The day after the allegations Kristine texted me. "We're not doing enough. One week of consent isn't enough. We need to make sure consent is a part of our culture from day one and every day after."

Of course we should. Of course we will. Now we just need to figure out how.

MAY

STUDENT ACTIVISM

IN THE MONTHS AFTER THE STONEMAN Douglas shooting, students organized en masse all over the country. There were walkouts, demonstrations, protests, a movement organized by students, and some that were co-opted (and nearly ruined) by staff. In one of my former schools, teachers tried to set up an event in the school theater instead and stood in front trying to wave the students in. The students just kept walking, because students are better at this than we give them credit for.

While the walk-past/walkout was happening, my students were holding a walkout of their own. They made signs and marched around the city park that backs into our school. They gave short improvised speeches and sang songs together. They stood in a circle, sharing their fears and anger and disgust at a world that can't keep them safe at their own school. When students speak up, when they pull themselves away from the dating and Snapchat streaks and all the things they should care about long enough to address something, we should listen.

And that's the thing. Really. Love or hate student protest, love or hate the Second Amendment or the student activists who led the fight against the NRA in the past few years, the students in my classroom and the students I'm talking to in other schools are not walking out because it's trendy. They aren't protesting as an excuse to get out of science. They are tangibly scared about a shooter in their school.

On this day, this big walkout day, their fear and anger wouldn't let them go back to school. They had walked, they had chanted, they had cried and hugged and screamed, but they had felt (and were probably right) that they hadn't made anything really better.

The energy then. The energy outside in this circle of kids. My god. If the problem had been something that could be lifted or fought, somehow physically restrained in some way. If will were enough, or if the world were there listening, my god.

My money is on these kids.

But also, of course, they are still kids. So when they decided they couldn't just stand there and couldn't just go back, that they had to move forward from the spot they had found, and when they decided that, yes, they would march to the state capitol, that day, right then, they didn't stop to make sure that legislators would be in session. They were not. They also didn't stop for directions, and so turned right after leaving the parking lot, though the capitol was to the left.

My principal, Ms. Kujawski, ran after them, pulled the students together who were obviously leading the thing, and tried to problem-solve. It's worth noting at this point that previous to this event, and many times after, I've heard students talk about planning protests or actions that may disrupt the school day, and when they've talked about the need for an element of surprise, or at the very least for the need to cut grown-ups out of knowing, they nearly always have said, "Except Ms. Kujawski" and then got a lot of "Well, yeah, obviously her," from the group. Kids trust her, kids know she has their back, kids know she will help them find their own voice.

Some of that trust can go a little too far, like when the students were mad at Ms. Kujawski for not being able to call a bus company, right then, and get themselves transported without notice, parent approval, or planning to the capitol building to stay until, you know, gun control happened. She talked them down, but only just. They absolutely would not head into class and were threatening quite believably to just start walking, most likely to shut down a nearby street or something (actions that are all well and good for adults during adult time, but less so for middle school kids during school hours).

They struck an agreement, and it was touch and go there for awhile, but the student leaders finally agreed that if they were going to really get something done, they would need to spend some time planning. They were offered my classroom and the rest of the school day. My principal (can you tell I like my principal?) got my regular classes covered and moved them to the library so I could sit with this group of students. My job for the rest of the day was to sit at my desk, do a whole lot of shutting up, and occasionally answer a question when the students were wondering what grown-ups would do about whatever idea they were pushing. That's all I did for what was probably the best three school hours of my teaching career.

All the kids did was run a democratic meeting of more than forty people that ranged from sixth to eighth graders. In the time they had, they settled on a name, a mission, a social media strategy, a few small next steps, and a regular meeting schedule to help achieve a few much larger goals. So, yeah, they did all that. I contributed a couple of ideas when asked, but they were quickly discarded. I also stayed after school once a week for the rest of the year so they could meet in my room, but I cannot claim that I led anything or even advised. I barely even supervised.

This is for the best, because I'm not very good at running student groups. When I first showed up at the school, I was handed leadership of their student antiracism group, a group that would have fallen apart completely under my fake-ass leadership if it weren't for the continued real-ass leadership of two different groups of Black girls who absolutely will not let their school not get better. Those meetings were on Tuesdays, though, which is a day when it's a lot easier for me to stay late. The newly formed student group on gun control found that with practices and rehearsals and church nights and everything else, the only regular night they could find to gather was Friday.

Oh, and nearly every Friday I wished all day that they would cancel their meeting, because it was Friday and I didn't want to be at school anymore, and I wanted to have tater tots and beer, but every damn Friday they met, without fail, for months. By the end of each meeting, I was never sad to have stayed.

Near the end of the year, my school held a day full of fun activities that students could sign up for. There was a video game room, and sports to play outside, and board games and movies, and in the library an all-day teach-in about gun violence led by those kids. I watched the kids build this thing, and I kinda secretly worried it would fall apart, or be, I don't know, cute? Like, "Let's paint a mural about how guns at school are bad and kindness is good" kind of cute?

It wasn't cute. The student group broke into many different parts. Teaching groups picked an important segment of guns and gun violence, spent weeks reading and researching about it, and distilling the most important information into ten-minute stations that participants would circle through. They had a station on school safety measures that could be instituted, a station devoted to opposition research understanding the history of the NRA and how it operates in politics now. There were stations to research active legislation and another to write letters to state representatives. There was an agenda printed, and all the student leaders had roles to move things along, document them, and problem-solve. There were songs and poems and speeches that were moving and beautiful, giving balance and focus to all the hard data also floating around.

There were midday feedback forms about presentations to be filled out. Seriously. Feedback forms. And in the afternoon a state representative who had recently done a sit-in in the state house chambers in an attempt to encourage her colleagues to bring some gun safety bills to the floor was invited in to speak. Kids listened and, when the speech was over, given the chance to ask a professional politician questions skipped right past favorite color or what made you want to be a politician and right to, "What are the best ways that young people can make sure their voices are included in policy?" and "What do you think the impacts of door-knocking versus holding events are on growing a movement?"

Like, seriously, these kids.

They've since won awards for their work, which is ongoing. The leadership core that has stuck with it, that honestly did the lion's share of all the work from day one and was also pushing hardest to keep the energy and enthusiasm up to make the group something special and impactful, was in sixth grade during that first walkout. Core members were meeting with mayors and town councils and media and activist leaders during the summer and spent their seventh grade year keeping that fire going, making connections, not shying from the unglamorous organizing stuff and sharing the fancy accolades and attention. These kids also, during their Friday meetings, would sometimes devolve into giggles about people who liked each other and whose friend heard that their friend was going to ask that other friend to a dance, watching music videos and being kids, which is what all that work was trying to protect in the first place.

There's this one small group, the leaders of the leaders, who wear their leadership comfortably, whom I have watched on the phone with powerful adult people, rolling their eyes as Mayor Whoever starts trying to sell them whatever bullshit line they think will placate a kid—"Well, these things take time, but we're moving in the right direction and bit by bit"—and then answering with, "Me and my friends are worried about being killed for going to school tomorrow. What are you going to do now to help us?"

I've seen leaders like them before, and they nearly always become the organization that they lead. Because they can be relied on to finish whatever they start, they are relied on to finish everything, and they do it, and then people stop showing up because it's not really their thing anyway anymore, and it all falls apart. These young women, though, as sixth graders, were very intentional about not doing so. They made sure all voices, specifically those of other people of color in the room, were amplified and taken seriously by all in attendance.

And also they really like Marvel movies and very bad bands and gossip and drama, and though the world needs them and all young leaders like them, I see every break they take, long or short, from fixing problems adults made, as a win for kids who still get to be kids.

They are who I think of when I think of Ollie's instinct for leadership and action. Ollie, like many young activists I have met and worked with, seems naturally intersectional in their action and thought. A good many of the leaders in the gun-control group are also active in the antiracism student group and our school's GSA. At meetings for one they bring in missions and goals of the other, but more than that, and more than the adults in the rooms of all those things, they don't see the goals and work as separate.

I credit the internet for making these kids so damn good at this, for giving them access to the best thinking happening instantly. I blame the lack of the internet for making me have to be a fake Buddhist and fake Communist and fake Republican before I started to figure out who I really am. It has helped my students learn and evolve and make connections at a level that wasn't accessible to young people before now. It's also where Ollie got to hear people they really thought were cool, mainly art and gaming YouTubers, talk about gender fluidity and identity. It's where Ollie, from a very young age, knew they weren't alone in how they felt, knew they deserved to be comfortable and safe.

I do a fair amount of work with pre-service teachers. A few months into fall semester, one approached me with a request. They had been talking with a few other people in their cohort, colleagues who identified as queer, gender-nonconforming, and trans. They had asked one of their professors how to go about navigating their personal identities in professional spaces. Like, how do you come out at school? Their professor told them, essentially, not to. He said they should hide it.

For a lot of reasons, this is a pretty fucked answer. How does a gender-nonconforming person hide that? Do they start performing a gender they are not in order to make others comfortable? Slap on some ill-fitting khakis and golf shirts and pretend to be, like, half the male social studies teachers I've ever seen? Do they hide who they love and live with? Anyone in a position to teach teachers should know that an essential element of doing this work well is being honest and present with your students. So not only was he asking them to live a lie, he was asking them to be mediocre teachers living a lie. We can and should do a whole lot better than that.

This group, then, looking for mentors, emailed me. To be clear, they did not want me to be their mentor. They are young, not stupid. They hoped that maybe I would know some LGBTQIA+ teachers, though, some who may want to sit and talk with them about the path ahead. So I did a little matchmaking, and things grew like they grow, and the group ended up putting on an event with a panel of out teachers and principals, a few speakers, and a bit of free wine and beer and packaged cookies.

A couple of weeks out from the event, I told Olive about it, told them that there would be people there who were nonbinary and heading into teaching, and asked if they wanted to come along. "Yes," they said without pausing, even though this would be a place with people and sitting and talking and all the things they usually hate. Then they paused for a second and asked, "Can I give a speech?"

In school Ollie's class had been working on persuasive speeches, with topics of each student's choosing. Ollie was working on a speech in class about gender identity and pronouns. They thought it would be pretty cool to share it with a bunch of teachers. The college kids were excited about it, even asked to do a quick Q&A with Ollie after about what they should know as teachers. I got to introduce Ollie to two of the main organizers of the event, future teachers who were both nonbinary. Ollie was so excited at the idea that they could someday have a teacher who was nonbinary. The two teachers were excited to meet a kid already so comfortable with who they are.

These kinds of moments could happen much more often, and that would be okay.

We ended up filling the room that night with forty or fifty people with clear plastic cups of box wine, gathered at tables and standing against the wall in a loose semicircle with chairs and a microphone set up in the middle.

Ollie, a third grader, stood in front of a room where the next youngest person was, like, twenty-three and just about to start a career in teaching, where other members of the audience had just talked about their decades and decades in school leadership. Ollie balanced their school Chromebook on a music stand, pointed the microphone down to their mouth, and gave this speech.

I love it when people ask, "What are your pronouns?" or "What do you identify as?" not "Are you a boy or a girl?" even though I love the surprise on their faces when I plainly say, "No." The only reason I care is that I don't want to explain every, single, time. People need to understand gender, it can change. We aren't changing shape, we are changing gender. People need to understand that gender ≠ geometry. I'm not a triangle. I'm Olive! I use they/them pronouns, I like blue (doesn't make me a boy), and I occasionally wear rainbows (doesn't make me a girl).

People have a choice on gender, not on others' but on theirs. You want to identify as a girl? Sure! A boy? Sure! A doggo? Maybe! And for pronouns. As you can guess, there is an abundance of them. Like Zie/Zir, Sie/Hir, and obviously the most used He/him, She/her, and they/them. You can be a girl and use He/Him, or a boy that uses She/Her. All that matters is that you feel comfortable with your pronouns. Not anyone else. Just don't let people go away misinformed, telling everyone they know that they met someone "weird." Explaining is the only way to have everyone be educated.

Make sure not to call anyone any pronouns they don't prefer. I know it can be hard remembering their pronouns. I sometimes forget my friend's pronouns, but I at least try to remember, and I try my best to correct myself. Just, generally, don't be rude about it, and assume that no one would fake it for attention. I'm not saying the future is fake, am I? People can be who they want to be, not who you want them to be. People have a choice on gender, not on others' but on theirs, theirs.

One time, I was washing my hands in the bathroom (the girl's bathroom), and a kid called me "weird." I guess that they thought that I was a boy because of my short hair. At least their mom was nice enough to apologize, but I bet that kid walked away confused, very. All of their life they were taught gender stereotypes, and then got an awkward reaction from their parents when they called someone (who they thought was a boy) in the girl's bathroom weird!

*Drop those gender stereotypes, not gently, **smash them! Right on the floor! Crush them on the floor!** Okay, I may have gotten a bit carried away there. I hate when people (especially*

*teachers) sort people by boys and girls. I don't know what wa-
ter fountain to go to! And I can't pick between being a boy or a
girl! That's why I'm nonbinary. Do you expect me to just go, "I'm
a girl now" to drink water! Water! So, just, can you not!*

*You know when video games ask, "Are you a boy or girl?"
that's the only time I cannot just say, "No." They sometimes
have different hairstyles or outfits for male or female characters. Girls have dresses, boys have pants or shorts. That seems
to be how our society works, even though it's not. People are
people, no matter what game, or place, people are people.*

*In school or other places, even if you don't get misgendered,
you should stand up for people who do. I do not like it when
those people just sit around when other people are either mis-
treating or being mistreated. Even though she tried to remember my pronouns, my old teacher just kinda sat there, while
people weren't being, you know, the best human beings.*

*All that I ask is that you aren't the person who tries to sit
next to someone at lunch just to tell them that their gender is
a lie! Just, don't be. It's so much easier and nicer to ask, "What
do you identify as?"*

Anyone who has spent time with teachers know they only really listen when young people are talking. While Ollie spoke, the
room was silent, still. There were no phones, no whispers. It was
silent in a way that people even muffled their loudest thoughts for
a few moments. And then it was over, and Ollie closed their laptop
and was embraced in applause and appreciation, and in one more
group of people in the world, I would forever be Ollie's dad before
I was anything else.

JUNE

THE MOST-RIGHT THING

DAD HAD BEEN DYING FOR AWHILE, BUT in a slow sort of way, slow enough to start to feel normal, like dying was more of a state of being than a process, like maybe he would be dying until he was very old, maybe just dying forever. But things sped up at the very end of the summer, and we knew that somehow, sometime soon, that impossible thing was going to happen, and he wouldn't be dying anymore.

I was with Dad at one of the very last doctor visits. We were talking with his doctor, this man who had shepherded him through years and years of cancer. Leukemia was shutting down Dad's kidneys. Sooner or later, the doctor said, but very likely sooner, we would come to the end. The doctor cried a little bit, sitting knee to knee with Dad. He told me and my brothers later that in his work it was very rare to treat someone so consistently for so long, that he had grown to really like him. Dr. Chitambar and the nurses who work with him are the very closest thing to saints recognized in my family.

The doctor left us to grab some tests, and I sat alone with my dad in the quiet nothing of the exam room. I tried to focus on this next procedure, this thing that would release some of the pressure in his kidneys, at least provide some comfort, but maybe even help treatment work better for awhile.

"The one thing I keep thinking about dying," my dad said, in that fatherly-like voice, his eyes trained hard on the wall in front of him, "is that I know a lot of people who have done it, so I'm pretty sure I can handle it."

I had nothing to say to that, except to put my hand on his shoulder. I think about that a lot still, and more than any of the talk of afterlives or stardust or becoming trees, it is, far and away, the most comforting thought I've ever heard about death.

This was fifteen years ago now. I was in my teacher training program, taking my last three-hour final of the summer, knowing I'd be driving to Dad's place in Wisconsin immediately after. The final was on a Saturday at 7 a.m., scheduled at that time, I think, because someone assumed that maybe a summer of ten-hour days learning educational history and theory wasn't torture enough. It was pouring outside, and the rain and the weekend and the summer meant that the class taking this final were the only people in the building, maybe the only ones on campus. Or, it felt like it anyway, until about five minutes after the exam started and a young man who had made many perplexing decisions about his own life started practicing his bagpipes just outside of our window. In the rain. Early on a Saturday morning.

I did not know it then, but I should have taken this as the first hint that my life was going to be surreal for a good long while. I would make it home for a visit, and Becca would come down a week later for the weekend. The idea was to give me a break from all the heaviness, so we told each set of our parents we were staying with the other, sneaking away like it was high school and getting a hotel room, but we ended up spending most of the night watching images come in of Hurricane Katrina's landfall as the Superdome filled and it seemed like maybe we were about to lose an entire American city. The rest of the time down there I spent with Dad, trying not to talk about how we were maybe about to lose him too. I left Dad's the day before class started up again, this last-time-seeing day punctuated by a hug goodbye that we both held a beat longer than we usually hold hugs, and when I started to release, Dad only held tighter.

I walked to the car where Becca was waiting to drive, sat next to her, and sobbed because I knew that he knew it would likely be our last time.

Dad would die about two weeks later, would be gone and gone and gone.

Before he died, right before this last big hug he gave me that I can still kinda feel if I try hard, my dad told me that it was us, his kids, that were the thing in his life he was the most proud of, the thing that went the most right. A decade and change later, I know exactly what Dad meant and can only torture myself wondering how much prouder he would have been had he lived to see the most-right thing in my life.

I know he would have gotten a huge kick out of Ollie's sense of humor, which can be dry and sarcastic like mine, but can also find ridiculous, over-the-top delight in small mistakes in the world like a sign that is misprinted, or autocorrect fails, or pictures of poorly baked cakes. Ollie shares these with Becca, and they laugh at little misfortunes, and I laugh at how hard they laugh together. Dad would have laughed at that too, just happy to see other people happy.

He has been gone long enough now that I can say he wasn't that good of a dad while we were young. He smoked a lot of weed, played a lot of disc golf, lost a lot of jobs, was generally and genuinely angry at a world that had not delivered him the upper-middle-class life he felt he was owed. Like a lot of bad dads out there, he left most of the actual raising of the kids to my mom, swooping in now and again for the fun stuff, swooping back out when we got obnoxious. (There were four of us a total of five years apart. We were often obnoxious.) When he and mom divorced and went to court, mom asked for the kids. Dad asked for his stereo.

His cancer fixed a lot of things. Faced with massive medical bills and the side effects of treatment, Dad lost the ability to make the money he needed to live. He fell back on our social safety nets and found himself thankful and reflective about the life he wanted to live with whatever time was left. He threw himself into small, attainable pleasures. He went on walks with his kids, drank dark German beer, started smoking better weed. Dad mellowed in ways that had nothing to do with his chronic fatigue, and it was in those years that I learned the most from him about what is truly important.

And now I have this Olive, this most-right thing about my life, this best thing I've ever been a part of. Raising Olive is most of what I think about, most of what Becca and I talk about when we're together, most of what I worry about, and is the source of most of my favorite moments of the past many years. I don't suppose that the raising of any kid is a normal thing, but Olive is . . . well . . . extra.

In the summer after Ollie's first year at the new school, we were looking at all the options for daily summer camps again. It was the same old stuff, and Ollie was really not interested in going to a lot of them. I'd taught hard all year and wrote a whole bunch, too, and wanted to do nothing more than spend my summer restaining a deck and ignoring everything else (even though I had no idea what I was doing). It would be helpful, I knew, to be able to drop Ollie off at a camp somewhere that would keep them occupied while I, you know, sanded or whatever. But also, Ollie was pretty self-sufficient around the house as long as they didn't need food or water or a charger for something or anything for any reason. I didn't push the camps that hard, still.

"I just wish we could do summer camp here," Ollie said, "like with just my friends." As I responded that we could think about it (which everyone knew meant that, yes, of course we were doing it), I knew it was also a god-awful idea. I mean (the part of me still looking at ten weeks of summer as an infinite source of time and adventure figured), one week doing stuff around the house with a bunch of pre-pre-teens would be just fine, maybe even cute or fun or something. Hey (the truly dumb part of me thought), they may well just keep each other busy enough that I'll have whole parts of the day to myself.

At camp, we ended up with mostly kids from Ollie's new school class, as well as the kid of famous writer guy. Most days we had seven or eight kids show up, some coming early because parents had to work and some leaving late for the same reasons, and so I had extra kids in my house every day for ten or eleven hours for a week. Mostly, I can say that it was wonderful. Also, mostly I can say that anyone teaching elementary school on purpose is a better person and teacher than I will ever be.

Ollie was amazing the whole time. For the month leading up to camp, Ollie started a Google doc between us and spent hours going over possible schedules for the day, activities we may or may not want to do, and was especially delighted to set the ground rules for how things would work. After all that work, we had a pretty strict schedule we were going to follow.

The plan was that we'd start every day (we didn't) with a little free-writing in journals we'd use throughout the day (we didn't). We would spend some time sharing our writing (just the first day) and maybe pick some to workshop into larger pieces (never happened). After writing, we would do our first activity, like building model rockets. (This mostly happened, though the kids all spent more time designing and printing flags to go on the side of the rockets, which, when launched, gave a great experiential, and somewhat dangerous, lesson on why NASA doesn't put huge flags on the sides of their rockets.)

There would be a lunch break with either an outside recess (hottest week of the year, nope), or if weather demanded, inside video game playing (every day, multiple times a day). There would be some open creation time after lunch with cardboard and paint and hot glue and stuff. (Somehow with only seven kids and two of them usually still playing video games, I could have used at least twelve more adults to help cut something or pour paint or clean paint off the thing that shouldn't be painted or whatever.) After we (hahahahaha) cleaned up, kids could chill and read for a while (mostly happened) before pickup time.

There were more successes than failures. The rocket launch was fun and hilarious. Cool art got made. One day Dr. LeeAnn Stephens, probably the best educator our state has ever seen, drove all the way over and showed the kids how to make ice cream in a bag just because she's an angel. We planned out most of a whole play that involved superpowers and alternate dimensions and an attack cat. The bad guy was played by a lime that was found in the kitchen and found again months later in the basement, tucked between some costumes, no longer the color of a lime. We tried to film the play on the last day, but also we were tired and also . . . Super Smash Bros. We got most of it done, enough to feel good about.

When the last kid left each day, I'd walk around my basement, clear stuff off the little stage I built for the room down there, take out the snack garbage, and have moments that felt very much like organizing the classroom at the end of a pretty good day.

The biggest thing, though, much bigger than anything that happened that week, was how different that week was for Ollie than it would have been a year before. Ollie is so much more relaxed, so much more confident and comfortable. In the past year, they have lived so completely as themselves, supported by a broad network of family, friends, and school. In the past year, they have made friends who think like they do, who feel and react like they do. Olive is happy so much more often than not, is creative and creating, is speaking up and being listened to.

A few days ago, Olive asked if I'd go for a bike ride. We rode on sidewalks mostly, and they stopped to look at every dog, noticed every yard sign and bumper sticker, commented on gardens and fences and porches. Riding a few feet in front of me, they talked the entire time, the wind only wiping away every third word or so. They talked about how the Japanese word for hair, god, and paper is all the same word, about how beta testing for a new video game was starting soon, about how they were doing this project where they were taking one of their drawings and trying to redo it in the style of different online artists, and they asked if anything was happening in the news (they ask me this at least once a day now), and they asked why it was happening, and had anything like that ever happened before, and if other people would say that something different was happening, and how those people would feel knowing the news was saying something different.

They talked and talked as we rode a wide circle around our neighborhood. I listened, even when I couldn't really hear. I'm doing my best to soak in these last years benefiting from the lessons of raising this kid. In not that many years, Ollie will be a teenager, and I'll have to start all over again.

ACKNOWLEDGMENTS

THIS BOOK WOULD HAVE BEEN A LOT less good without the early reading help of Kara, Maire, and Amy, not to mention the constant vision and work of Erik. I would have been a lot less good of a person without the friendship, leadership, and thinking of Nate and LeeAnn and Shanna and Alexei and Alison and Maya and Mandy and Sydney. I would have died long ago, surrounded in my own filth and sadness, without my family, especially my wife and kid.

TOM RADEMACHER is an English teacher and the author of *It Won't Be Easy: An Exceedingly Honest (and Slightly Unprofessional) Love Letter to Teaching* (Minnesota, 2017). His writing has been published in the *Huffington Post, EdPost,* and *MinnPost.* In 2014 he was honored as Minnesota's Teacher of the Year.